THE END OF HOPE—THE BEGINNING

THE END OF HOPE—THE BEGINNING

NARRATIVES OF HOPE IN THE FACE OF DEATH AND TRAUMA

PAMELA R. MCCARROLL

Fortress Press
Minneapolis

THE END OF HOPE—THE BEGINNING

Narratives of Hope in the Face of Death and Trauma

Cover Image © Thinkstock

Cover design: Erica Rieck

Library of Congress Cataloging-in-Publication Data

Print ISBN: 978-0-8006-9966-6

eBook ISBN: 978-1-4514-4192-5

The paper used in this publication meets the minimum requirements of American National Standard for Information Sciences — Permanence of Paper for Printed Library Materials, ANSI Z329.48-1984.

Manufactured in the U.S.A.

This book was produced using PressBooks.com, and PDF rendering was done by PrinceXML.

CONTENTS

Acknowledgments

As with all projects of this kind, many people have been part of it coming to fruition. First, I am grateful to the people whose lives have inspired this book and borne witness to hope's hidden horizons of possibility in the face of devastating loss. These people include patients, congregants, students, families, and caregivers, all of whom through struggle have found new ways to trust, persevere, and stay committed to life amid the pull to death. While I know the depth and breadth of lived human experience cannot find full expression in words on a page, in humility and gratitude I offer written words about their life stories, trusting that something of hope's horizons of possibility can be glimpsed through them. Thank you especially to those who read specific chapters and engaged them from their own experiences of care, loss, death, and trauma.

I am grateful to Principal Dorcas Gordon and the board of Knox College, whose thoughtful leadership and gracious support for research have enabled time and quiet space for this manuscript to be conceived and written. Many thanks go to Douglas and Rhoda Hall for their intellectual and spiritual inspiration and ongoing support. I am indebted to my early CPE supervisor, John O'Connor, whose teaching on hope in clinical contexts engaged my imagination and fed my clinical practice. I am grateful to the people and leadership of St. Andrew's Presbyterian Church in Toronto and particularly to the Rev. Dr. George Vais, whose invitation to provide a lecture series inspired the seeds and framework for this book. Much appreciation goes to Susan MacLeod and the Vais family for their gracious support for this work. I extend gracious thanks to my students, my colleagues at Knox College and the Toronto School of Theology, those within the Presbytery of East Toronto and the CPE supervisor group, and the people of St. Mark's Presbyterian Church in Toronto. Among these communities, I have experienced the struggle and commitment to reach toward transcendent possibility in the face of trials and tribulations. These communities have inspired me and given me much food for the journey.

I am grateful to Kay Diviney for her thoughtful and incisive editorial work on chapter 2 and her willingness to have her holiday interrupted by my editorial needs. Kay's many skills in editing, writing, and theological thought have been a great gift to me. Many thanks go to Helen Cheung, whose extensive research contributed to the inductive literature review presented in chapter 2. As well,

I am appreciative of Will Bergkamp and the people of Fortress Press, whose commitment to excellence in Christian publishing has brought forth many outstanding books and continues to serve the ongoing formation of Christian thought, identity, spirituality, and engagement in the North American context. Their willingness to work with me on this project has inspired its timely completion. It is a privilege to work with them.

I extend gratitude to my friends and family: to Sue Koziey-Kronas for her authenticity, honesty, and willingness to allow me alongside her on the journey; to Ben, Caleb, Mark, and Hannah, whose lives continue to inspire and ground me; to Paul and Kath, whose ongoing support and generosity in sharing "the cottage" enabled time away to read, ponder, and write; to Harris, who has partnered with me through this project, reading and rereading every word and whose huge mind and heart for theology and ministry bear much fruit in these pages and in the shared story of our lives. Finally, I extend prayers of thanksgiving to the One within whose horizon we participate, whose hidden and gracious presence amid the adversities of life and whose ongoing call to trust and live without excuse bring me to my knees in humility and gratitude again and again.

Toronto, September 1, 2013

Introduction

Hoping against Hope

This book is about hope. In particular, it is about the presence and possibility of hope in the face of endings, in the face of death and trauma, in the face of the unalterable and unwanted crises in life. The bulk of the book explores diverse narratives of hope in which the recognizable yet mysterious presence of hope is intimated in the face of traumatic loss and death. We consider manifestations of hope that have emerged from the stories of people speaking from palliative-care beds and emergency rooms, from wheelchairs and long-term care facilities. In working with people facing death and traumatic loss, I have come to agree with William Stringfellow when he stresses, "Hope is known only in the midst of coping with death. Any so-called hope is delusionary and false apart from the confrontation with the power of death."[1] Thus, it is in the face of such extremity of being and death that we dig deeply to seek out narratives of hope that emerge at the edge of the horizon of life's possibility.

Before presenting the goals and outline of the book, I share here my primary location in this exploration of hope. While doing research in constructive-systematic theology on the crisis of hope through the lens of a contextual theology of the cross,[2] I was also serving as a chaplain and educator in a large teaching hospital.[3] Many of the patients, families, caregivers, and students with whom I worked faced questions of hope and hopelessness every day. They included people in palliative care who were living their dying, survivors of trauma whose lives were stopped cold by sudden accident and violence, caregivers who yearned to find a means to hope in the face of extreme and multiple tragedies, and students who wrestled with questions of pastoral

1. William Stringfellow, *An Ethic for Christians and Other Aliens in a Strange Land* (Waco, TX: Word, 1973), 138.

2. See Pamela R. McCarroll, *Waiting at the Foot of the Cross: Toward a Theology of Hope for Today* (Eugene, OR: Pickwick, 2014).

3. *Spiritual care practitioner* is now the preferred name for chaplain in health care settings in Canada. However, for the sake of clarity, I will use the term *chaplain* throughout the book. In my capacity as an educator, I worked interprofessionally with other health care disciplines and as a clinical pastoral education (CPE) supervisor with groups of students training at the basic, advanced, and specialist levels.

identity and with how to hope when fix-it solutions were not available. As I struggled to write systematically about ideas of hope and hopelessness in my research, I found myself in the midst of experiences that, in devastating and profound ways, caused me to pause and to pay attention. How do we hope at the end of hope? These patients, families, caregivers, and students became interlocutors for me, inviting me to see the many faces of hope in the midst of crisis and death. Bearing witness to the multidimensionality of hope in these people and their stories has opened up for me the scriptural narratives and theological renderings of hope in new and revitalized ways.

While it is located within the discipline of pastoral theology, this book is an exercise in practical theology, as it brings into dialogue concrete human experiences with theology, the Scriptures, philosophy, and health care research so as to serve the deepening of the spiritual life, theological thought, and practices of care in the face of suffering.[4] In collecting and writing people's stories, I have drawn on qualitative methods of research for many chapters in this book (chapters 3 to 7). As a participant observer and through field notes, interviews, and textual material, I have recorded the narratives of several individuals and families in the face of trauma and death. As much as possible, I have invited the individuals, families, and caregivers to reflect on the stories both to ensure accuracy and to enable the research process itself to serve transformative possibility in their lives. I carry a deep appreciation for qualitative methods of research and the extent to which lived human experience is held up as the focus of study and as a source of wisdom. Further, I appreciate the extent to which qualitative (and quantitative) methods can serve improved practice and can have therapeutic outcomes for participants, feeding a sense of purpose and meaning in the face of adversity. However, I count myself as part of an emerging group of pastoral theologians who respectfully challenge the propensity within the discipline to prioritize social sciences over theology.[5] While I affirm that there are important dialogues that need to take place between theology and the social sciences and that some social scientific methods

---

4. See Peggy Way, *Created by God: Pastoral Care for All God's People* (St. Louis, Chalice, 2005); Sharon G. Thornton, *Broken yet Beloved* (St. Louis: Chalice, 2002); Pamela Cooper-White, "Suffering," in *The Wiley-Blackwell Companion to Practical Theology*, ed. Bonnie Miller-McLemore (East Sussex, UK: Wiley, 2012), 23–31. Way, Thornton, and Cooper-White identify that pastoral theology has suffering as its starting point. Pastoral theology is, therefore, focused on responses to the reality of suffering in life.

5. See, for example, Russell Herbert, "Introduction: The Importance of Hope," in *Living Hope: A Practical Theology of Hope for the Dying* (Werrington, UK: Epworth, 2006) , 1–14; Thornton, introduction to *Broken yet Beloved*, 1–4; Stanley J. Grenz, "The Hopeful Pessimist: Christian Pastoral Theology in a Pessimistic Context," *Journal of Pastoral Care* 54 (2000): 297–322.

allow space for theological commitments to be central, I am concerned that several social scientific methods eclipse transcendence from ways of knowing and, as such, do not provide an appropriate ground for pastoral theology.

As a pastoral and practical theologian, I begin with lived theology and with particular faith commitments to the Creator revealed in Jesus and mediated in the world by the Spirit. The essence of God is love; thus, the experience of love[6] reflects the presence and power of God. My perspectives on the world have been deeply influenced by a theology of the cross. Viewed from that position, expressions of glory—of triumphalism and power, of unmitigated positivism, optimism, and success, and so on—are considered suspect, requiring critique and deconstruction. In a theology of the cross, experiences of suffering, failure, vulnerability, and limit are held up as contexts where hidden truth may be revealed. Indeed, in focusing on experiences of death and trauma as the context out of which authentic hope may be found, I follow a "method of the cross."[7] My theological commitments shape my understanding of who we are and what we are made for—creatures made by love and for love in contexts where love's presence and possibility are most often hidden and distorted.

Following ancient ways of thought,[8] a priority on love shapes my epistemology, which affirms that the deepest knowing or knowledge of a thing comes with the enlightening of love.[9] Rather than things being solely known as objects to be examined by reason and research methods common to modern science, deeper knowing comes with the enlightening of love wherein a thing's beauty or belovedness is glimpsed. This is not to say that there is not a place for reason or quantitative and qualitative research methods in practical and pastoral theology. However, it does mean that these methods are intended to serve the deepening of love and awe, rather than the opposite. This epistemology presupposes that the illumination by love is the goal of knowledge. It affirms that love's source is transcendent while its presence is experienced in the real

6. Here, love is considered to be manifestated in many recognizable experiences and actions--compassion, forgiveness, respect, justice and peacemaking, a sense of awe and so on.

7. See McCarroll, "Part 1: The Method of the Cross as Waiting," in *Waiting at the Foot of the Cross*, 27-88.

8. In ancient sources, including the Hebrew Scriptures and philosophers of antiquity, loving and knowing were deeply intertwined. One could not truly know a thing without loving it. For more on this, please see George Grant, "Faith and the Multiversity," in *Technology and Justice* (Toronto: Anansi, 1986), 36–77.

9. In several places, Simone Weil describes the importance of the enlightening or illumination of love for true knowledge of things. Please see Simone Weil, *Formative Writings, 1929–1941*, ed. and trans. Dorothy Tuck McFarland and Wilhelmina Van Ness (London: Routledge & Kegan Paul, 1987). Weil's thought influences my epistemology.

world of relationships as a movement of energy among and between humans and in creation. Love is what recognizes the essential *imago dei*, the essential beauty of a thing, as a creation of the Divine. Love honors difference and particularity without fear; love pays attention and waits upon the hidden beauty of a thing to be revealed; love seeks to deconstruct and resist the tragic and oppressive blocks that mar and hide the possibilities for creaturely belovedness to flourish. Given all this, the following practices have been central to my chaplaincy work and to the narrative priorities of this project: deep listening, focused attention, and waiting upon the illumination of love (Weil). These practices have shaped the way I have sought to be with people in the face of trauma and death even when I have failed miserably. They have shaped the way I have borne witness to the sometimes unlikely narratives of hope that emerged from hospital beds and from the stories shared in these pages.

This book seeks to demonstrate multiple ways to recognize the presence of hope in human stories especially in the face of trauma and death. I present these narratives of hope as a response to the crisis of hope that emerges in the face of endings (on individual, collective, and societal levels) and as an invitation to more profound recognition of the presence and possibility of hope in our midst. The narratives shared here are not exhaustive, but rather invitational, that we might continue to seek out the unique and unexpected ways that hope is present in human life. My goal is fourfold: First, I seek to open up space and to complexify understandings of hope wherein plurality and diversity can exist. It is through such complexity that we most honor our existence as creatures—embedded within creation, unable to know reality in totality, yet given glimpses of a larger whole within which we exist. Second, I present these narratives with the role of the caregiver in mind. What does it mean to provide care in contexts of crisis and death, when hope is at its end? How do we take seriously the call to witness to hope as caregivers, pastors, and chaplains in ways that fully enter the darkness of human experience and hopelessness? Third, central to my project is a desire to bring into dialogue the emergency room and the Scriptures, the deathbed and a cruciform faith. How can these sources speak to each other and draw forth multiple ways to discern the presence and possibility of hope as it moves in human lives? Finally, a background interest of this book is to begin to consider how these multiple narratives of hope may suggest certain practices in response to the crisis of hope that dominates many mainline churches in North America at the end of church as it has been known.

In chapter 1, I provide a brief sociocultural-historical discussion of hope as it has been construed within the modern West, especially in the North American context. While I have written on this extensively elsewhere,[10] this brief chapter locates our discussion on hope within a broader framework and helps illuminate the larger crisis of hope that impinges upon and frames the contemporary experience of hope in human relationships and life journeys. As well, in highlighting the crisis of hope that has emerged in the modern West, this discussion helps to illustrate the need to further broaden our understanding of hope and to recognize anew unexpected manifestations of hope in the face of endings.

The second chapter is an extensive review of the pastoral and practical theological literature on hope over thirty-five years (1976–2011). While this chapter is lengthy, it helps to provide a general landscape of the dominant themes and tensions present in the understandings of hope in the field. It examines hope within these disciplines with reference to much of the secondary literature within multiple other disciplines, including psychology, health care research, philosophy, and systematic and biblical theology, all of which influence working understandings of hope in pastoral and practical theology. The chapter ends by presenting a descriptive definition of hope that is inclusive of all the many different emphases and tensions present in discussions on hope within a large and diverse body of literature. This definition becomes a central area of exploration in the chapters that follow.

Chapters 3 to 7 explore five different narratives of hope: hope as fight, hope as meaning, hope as survival, hope as lament, and hope as surrender. Each of these chapters presents a story that is based on experiences of people with whom I have worked or whom I have known in the hospital, congregational, or church context. In all cases, except when the story has been published,[11] names and details have been changed so as to ensure confidentiality. Further, as mentioned previously, where possible, individuals involved in the cases have reviewed the material, given permission for its use, and added changes and suggestions to the text. In each of these chapters, the narratives are explored inductively in relation to the specific theme of the chapter, in terms of the descriptive definition of hope and in terms of practices of care. Finally, following the inductive discussion, each chapter focuses on the respective theme of hope in relation to the larger body of literature. We consider how each narrative can feed hope and what this means for caregivers, pastors, chaplains, and all those called to bear witness to hope. These five different narratives of hope are intended to be invitational explorations of hope's presence and possibilities in the midst of contexts in which hope is least expected.

10. See McCarroll, *Waiting at the Foot of the Cross.*

11. Chapter 7, "Hope as Surrender," is based on the book, used with permission, Chris Vais, *For Words: A Journal of Hope and Healing* (Guelph, ON: Susan McLeod, 2003).

The concluding chapter summarizes some areas for further exploration and concludes by raising questions about what these narratives and this working definition of hope might suggest for further nurturance of hope in pastoral practice. Finally, it points to possibilities for churches in decline. How might broader perspectives on hope open up multiple ways to nourish and enact hope in Christian communities that exist at the end of church as it has been known?

This book is intended to feed hope in a way that attends to the suffering and terror of life head-on, in a way that feeds hope's possibilities in human life and practices of care. In bringing together several different narratives of hope, I seek to open space for wondering, for meeting, for seeing anew the hidden possibilities in life. In honoring stories of people with whom I have worked, I bear witness to the absolute meaningfulness of life as it is lived in all its particularity—an offering of hope in the midst of difficult times. *The End of Hope—the Beginning*: as the paradoxical, open-ended title suggests, the way ahead is unknown, and the pathways are numerous. Such paradoxical open-endedness requires trust, courage, perseverance, and an eye for hidden possibility.

1

A Brief History of Hope in the Modern West

My generation has grown up in a world where the real possibility of massive destruction of the planet was plausible every day. As a child in the late 1960s and '70s, I would awaken each morning with a sense that it could be our last, for it all might disappear with one press of a button. Throughout my generation, the Doomsday Clock, now at five minutes to midnight,[1] has stood as a symbol of the time in which we live. It is a reminder of how close we are to self-inflicted global disaster and how powerless the average citizen feels to do much about it. It tells us that future destruction is just minutes away. Only through the stories of parents and grandparents can my generation imagine a planet without disaster hanging over it on a massive scale. Living in the context of such global threat is a truly novel phenomenon in history and raises many questions about the possibility to hope in a time such as ours. While other eras and contexts have faced struggles in purpose, meaning, and the possibility of hope, there is something new in the struggle to hope in the face of such global destructive possibilities, especially as this relates to the narrative of hope in the modern West.

What does hope mean these days when it is difficult to find our bearings in the present, much less in the future? What does hope mean when economies are collapsing, when more and more people live in poverty and violence, when our vulnerability as societies has been torn open by the unpredictability of terrorism, when helplessness in the face of the world's problems has become a way of life for many? How can we hope when there no longer seems to be a way for us to share dreams and to speak collectively about the possibilities for a better

---

1. The Doomsday Clock is a symbolic clock, overseen by the *Bulletin of the Atomic Scientists* at the University of Chicago. The most recent resetting, at five minutes to midnight, was made on January 14, 2013. See www.thebulletin.org.

future? Some have suggested that we have come to the end of hope: that people today have lost a sense of a transcendent vision for the future, a shared sense of meaning and a commitment to common ends. The larger institutions that formerly shaped our shared sense of identity, purpose, and meaning—the church and the governing bodies—no longer earn our trust. This loss, they argue, has resulted in an inability to hope.[2]

Related to this, we are at a time when cultural critics, postmodern thinkers, and increasingly the public at large are suspicious of metanarratives, the grand stories that seek to articulate a larger meaning within which we find ourselves. "That is not my experience," is a common refrain in reaction to perceived attempts to speak on behalf of any collective *we*. The concern is that metanarratives attempt to normalize human *experiences* into a universal human *experience* such that many people are rendered invisible, many voices are silenced. The postmodern critique of metanarratives grows from a commitment to resist the oppression of such totalizing narratives as this is played out in the stories we tell about ourselves—who we are and what we are made for. This rejection of metanarratives has been profoundly important for opening up space for people and communities to name and claim their own stories and meanings, and it powerfully resists oppressive ways of thinking, speaking, and being, but many believe this rejection also has profound implications for hope and hopelessness and how these are lived out in our midst.

Andrew Delbanco argues that "human beings need to organize inchoate sensations amid which we pass our days—pain, desire, pleasure, fear—into a story. When that story leads somewhere and helps to navigate through life to its inevitable terminus in death, it gives us hope. And if such a sustaining narrative establishes itself over time in the minds of a substantial number of people we call it culture."[3] Following Delbanco, Emily Griesinger and the authors whom she represents insist that narratives frame our sense of meaning and enable ways to interpret fundamental questions of existence: "Who am I? Why am I here? Given life's difficulties—evil, suffering, death—how shall I respond, act, live?"[4] Yet we find ourselves at a time when all narratives that seek to point to larger meanings and shared experience are viewed with suspicion and deconstructed before their meanings can be absorbed. How can hope exist when there is no way to understand our lives within a larger narrative than that of our own

2. See Emily Griesinger and Mark Eaton, eds., *The Gift of Story: Narrating Hope in a Postmodern World* (Waco, TX: Baylor University Press, 2006); Andrew Delbanco, *The Real American Dream: A Meditation on Hope* (Cambridge, MA: Harvard University Press, 1999).

3. Delbanco, *The Real American Dream*, 1.

4. Griesinger and Eaton, *The Gift of Story*, x.

making, when there is no means by which to shape shared expectancy into the future?

There are others who come at the failure of hope from a different perspective. They agree that hope has come to an end in modernity, but this failure, they argue, marks the end of a false version of hope and opens the possibility for truer and deeper hope to emerge. Douglas John Hall is persuasive in his insistence that the end of hope as is has been known in modernity actually opens up space for authentic hope to be discovered. Following Kierkegaard and others, Hall identifies the crisis of hope in terms of the relationship of present experience to future expectation. Since images of the future have been darkened by the threats under which we live, there is no way to see into the future, so there is no way to live with hope in the present. Hopelessness abounds precisely because we have no way to hope outside the narrative of modernity and its story of progress through human agency that guides us into the future. The fact that hope as espoused in the modern metanarrative has been found out (so to speak), he argues, is better than living in the falseness of modern hope that could never be realized. In deconstructing modernity's triumphalistic narrative of hope by way of the theology of the cross, he explores possibilities of true hope that emerge in the face of the fragility, vulnerability, and brokenness of human life and history.[5]

Some philosophers, theologians, and literary critics have tracked the emergence of the metanarrative of modernity.[6] Much has been made of modernity's shift away from premodern ways of seeing the world and how this has affected notions of hope as it is understood collectively. The general story of hope in the West goes something like this: With modernity, there was a gradual but vast shift away from the enchanted universe of premodernity and to scientific methods that prioritized what could be measured by humans. No longer was truth (or hope, for that matter) considered to reside in a transcendent dimension that was unknowable except by faith mediated through the church. In modernity, truth became accessible primarily through scientific

---

5. See Douglas John Hall, *Thinking the Faith: Christian Theology in a North American Context*, (Minneapolis: Fortress Press, 1989).

6. See, for example Richard Bauckham and Trevor Hart, *Hope against Hope: Christian Eschatology at the Turn of the Millennium* (Grand Rapids: Eerdmans, 1999); Delbanco, *The Real American Dream*; George Grant, *Time as History*, 1969 (Toronto: University of Toronto Press, 1995); Griesinger and Eaton, *The Gift of Story*; Hall, *Thinking the Faith*; Flora Keshgegian, *Time for Hope: Practices for Living in Today's World* (New York: Continuum International , 2006); Christopher Lasch, *The True and Only Heaven: Progress and Its Critics* (New York: Norton, 1991); Charles Taylor, *A Secular Age* (Cambridge, MA: Harvard University Press, 2007).

reason. Indeed, within modernity, there were some reactions to the prioritizing of reason over other aspects of human experience; in particular, some emphasized feeling,[7] and others doing.[8] But one way or the other, in modernity it became a given that truth could be *discovered* through human effort, ingenuity, and experience. This shift from premodernity to modernity has been described as a movement wherein the eternal transcendent dimension of premodernity was eclipsed from the knowing and experience of modern reality.[9] Religion—or understandings of reality that included dimensions beyond that which is perceivable, understandings of reality that bound the world together—was relegated to the private sphere, no longer part of shared public discourse or thought.

Scientific methods sought to demystify the world, seeking out truth that could be found by human abilities in facts that were waiting to be discovered. As human use of scientific reason developed, new things and new ways of using things were discovered. Gradually the world—once a place of fierce beauty, awe, and terror—came to be known primarily for the resources it offered for human consumption and comfort. Forests, lakes, rocks, and fields became valuable primarily as resources for human use through technology and science, not as part of creation, loved into being by a gracious Creator. Some have described this as the dominance of "technological reason,"[10] wherein the truth, beauty, and goodness of a thing could be understood only in terms of the thing's utility and usefulness. Human control and mastery over these things, now called *resources*, enabled science to manipulate nature in order to make new and better things that would enable human progress into the future. Human control and mastery over the human condition itself would also enable this progress.

What does this have to do with hope? Basically, with the modern eclipse of transcendence, notions of collective hope became associated with what is possible through human agency and mastery. Rather than hope being placed outside history, in a transcendent God who would make all things right at

7. Generally, in theological circles, Friedrich Schleiermacher is associated with the focus on feeling as an essential aspect of human experience through which humans can know and can access truth. He is embedded within the larger Romanticism movement of Europe during the late eighteenth and early nineteenth centuries. As well, he is an important part of the pietism movement within the Reformed German church of that time.

8. Generally, Karl Marx and other revolutionary movements are associated with a priority placed on action, doing, and making change happen.

9. See, for example, George Grant, *Philosophy in the Mass Age* (Toronto: University of Toronto Press, 1995, repr., 1959).

10. See, for example, George Grant, *Technology and Justice* (Toronto: Anansi, 1986). See also Jacques Ellul, *The Technological Society* (New York: Vintage, 1969).

the end of time, in heaven or in a renewed earth (as the case may be), hope was placed firmly in history and humanity's ability to make history happen—to create a better future. *Hope within history* meant that hope was considered to be a human-directed endeavor rather than a transcendent reality. It meant that hope would be powered by human dreams of the future that, in turn, would propel people forward in action. Hope's object was concrete, measurable, and outcome based. Hope's mechanism was human agency. Hope's means and assurance were mastery over human and nonhuman nature to bring the future into being.

Perhaps the most helpful shorthand way to unpack the relationship between hope and history as it has been construed in modernity is to draw on Karl Marx and his oft-cited critique of religion. Marx argued that religion functioned as the "opiate of the people."[11] What he meant by this is that with religion, humans place their hope in divine agency to grant eternal salvation in an afterlife, rather than placing hope in the power of people to change their circumstance in the here and now. He was particularly critical of the pie-in-the-sky promise of heavenly reward for earthly obedience, which kept people subservient to the powers that be and enabled oppression, suffering, and the status quo to continue unchecked. Marx, representing strong currents in modernity, sought to situate hope firmly in history, as the product and goal of human agency and desire to change the world.

Assumptions of progress became embedded within the modern narrative of hope. The philosopher Hegel is among those most commonly associated with giving voice to this notion of progress. Marx built on Hegel's work by emphasizing humans as agents and masters of history, rather than Hegel's spiritualized historicism that identified a Spirit-led progressive movement in history in which Spirit was working its purposes through humanity.[12] Modern ideas of hope in history imagined a progressive linear notion of time into the future wherein things would get better and better. Knowledge would build on knowledge, science on science, until we would create a world resembling something like heaven on earth or utopia. There was a sense of inevitability about it. What has been coined the "religion of progress"[13] enabled people to

11. This is a phrase coined by Marx in introduction to *A Contribution to a Critique of Hegel's Philosophy of Right*, in *German-French Annals* (Paris, Deutsch Französische Jahrbücher, 1844).

12. See G. W. F. Hegel, *Phenomenology of the Spirit*, trans. A. V. Miller with foreword and analysis by J. N. Findlay (Oxford: Oxford University Press, 1977).

13. See Harris Athanasiadis, *George Grant and the Theology of the Cross: The Christian Foundation of his Thought* (Toronto: University of Toronto Press, 2001), 141. George Grant and those influenced by Grant use the term "religion of progress" frequently to refer to the religion that plays the flatterer of modernity.

think of hope in terms of optimism—optimism about the future and optimism about the ends toward which human beings are capable.

Several thinkers, writing at the end of modernity, argue that the major problems with the modern narrative are manifested in its assumptions about who people are and what humans are made for, based on a universe without God.[14] Because the narrative is wrong about this, it cannot help but turn in on itself, which is something, they argue, we can see happening all around us, recognizable in the "data of despair".[15] The modern dream assumes an optimistic view of human nature and history and posits that humans exist to be masters of the world and that the goal of human life is to master and change the world, that it might more fully become what we want it to become—whether that means the kingdom of God, the perfect socialist state, or the ideal democracy. Because there was optimism about the human condition and history, it was appropriate to place hope in human and historical terms. It was not a problem for humans to be masters of the earth, because of the optimistic view of the human condition. It was not a problem for progress to be the natural way of history, because of the optimistic view of history. This identity as masters included the idea that all that exists is intended to be mastered by humans to be used for human purposes. Such purposes would inevitably feed the flourishing of all of life on the planet and beyond.

Some have noted that North America more than any other region in the world has internalized this modern dream in its self-understanding;[16] consequently, at the end of modernity, this region is facing a greater crisis with the fragmentation of this dream. This is particularly evident in the crisis of hope in North America. Part of the North American version of the modern dream is to see itself as the "New World" full of endless possibilities—a promised land. This New World mythology and the way it feeds modern notions of hope are perpetuated in every generation with the arrival of new immigrants and refugees seeking a better life. At the same time, however, the New World myth has been a powerful narrative that has silenced those who have not experienced a promised land: the first peoples, whose land and ways of life were stolen by those claiming it as the New World, and those brought to North American shores by force to work as slaves. The breaking down of the

14. Some examples include the work of Douglas John Hall, George Grant, Christopher Lasch, and others.

15. Douglas John Hall uses this term throughout his corpus. See for example, Douglas John Hall, *The Reality of the Gospel and the Unreality of the Churches* (Minneapolis: Fortress Press, 2007), 176.

16. See George Grant, "In Defence of North America," in *Technology and Empire* (Toronto: Anansi, 1969), 17–19; Keshgegian, *Time for Hope*, 11–12, 77ff.

dominant metanarrative has enabled other stories to come forward while also raising important questions as to the possibilities for shared narratives of hope in the North American context.

Certainly the history-making impulse of modernity to change the world has brought incredible benefits to many humans on several fronts: medical treatments, housing, access to water, electricity, and transportation. As well, this modern version of hope has inspired efforts to develop technologies and economic plans that seek to diminish suffering and to move toward a goal of human flourishing for all. This history-making spirit has opened up possibilities for democracy and how we govern ourselves. Yes, placing our hope in history and in the achievements of human agency has served many humans in many ways.

However, as the Doomsday Clock demonstrates, we also find ourselves in the second decade of the twenty-first century having lived the most violent of centuries, having produced the most violent of weapons, having ravaged the earth in ways that may be irreparable. The grand hopes of modernity's dream have been dashed by the massive suffering of the last century and by the oppressive silencing of many. Modernity's hope in human achievement has been crushed by the cries from gas and torture chambers, from refugee camps and war zones, from tar sands and nuclear meltdowns. The same history-making spirit that promised an end to suffering through human ingenuity and science has brought on suffering on a grander and more global scale. The metanarrative of hope in history has fallen in on itself, and we find ourselves as a species surrounded by the fragments of modernity's dream.

When hope is at its end, how then do we hope? This is a question to which many thinkers and people of faith have given their minds. As suggested earlier, Douglas Hall responds to this question by shifting the focus. He explores how the present experience of hopelessness marks the beginning of the possibility for authentic hope. For him and other theologians of the cross, the character of hope for our context is recognizable at the end of hope, waiting at the foot of the cross, trusting the One who brings new life unexpectedly when all hope is dead.[17]

---

17. Others who follow a similar argument include George Grant, *Technology and Justice*; Alan E. Lewis, *Between Cross and Resurrection: A Theology of Holy Saturday* (Grand Rapids: Eerdmans, 2001); Pamela R. McCarroll, *Waiting at the Foot of the Cross: Toward a Theology of Hope for Today* (Eugene, OR: Pickwick, 2014); Jürgen Moltmann, *The Theology of Hope*, trans. Margaret Kohl (London: SCM, 1965); Shelly Rambo, *Spirit and Trauma: A Theology of Remaining* (Louisville: Westminster John Knox, 2010); Sharon G. Thornton, *Broken yet Beloved: A Pastoral Theology of the Cross* (St. Louis: Chalice, 2002).

In considering the possibility of hope for today, Canadian theologian, activist and writer Mary Jo Leddy has described the situation something like this: In modernity, we thought history was a road map. Looking down, we saw the complete story—we could see where we were headed, and we knew how to get there. The road map showed us. Hope was pervasive. The road ahead was clear. Now we have discovered that we are not actually looking down from above, but rather we are embedded in the world, walking at night, without a road map, and we are not sure where we are heading. We have only a small flashlight that can show us where to place our next step, but that is it. Hope, she describes, is small but present in the light of the flashlights, the willingness to trust, to talk to each other, and to take steps in the dark.[18]

Philosopher Jonathan Lear in his book *Radical Hope* explores the character of hope through reflection on the life of Plenty Coups, the last chief of the Crow nation, at the time when everything fell apart and nothing made sense anymore. Lear considers the possibility of hope in the face of absolute abyss and cultural devastation of the Crow nation. Later in life, when Plenty Coups describes the destruction of the lives of his people, he says, "When the buffalo went away the hearts of my people fell to the ground and they could not lift them up again. After this," he says, "nothing happened."[19] It is precisely this point—that of a people faced with the end of their way of life—that prompts Lear's exploration of hope. "After this nothing happened." He asks, "How should we face the possibility that our civilization might collapse?"[20] How can we live with the meaning of this kind of vulnerability of the human condition? Lear considers hope as it exists invisibly beneath narratives of meaning, in the very beingness of what is and a waiting upon what will be. He considers how, in the face of cultural devastation and disorientation that is part of the experience of living today, we can draw from the life of Plenty Coups a way to hope in the face of the abyss and the devastation of life.

These images of hope conjure up some distinct though related elements regarding the character of hope for the living of these days: hope is seen in the posture of waiting at the foot of the cross, in a flashlight, in steps and conversation in the dark, in surviving and existing in the midst of abyss. All of these images of hope share a focus on trust and faith, on being and

---

18. Mary Jo Leddy's image is unpublished and presented as part of her lecture at the 2010 Kairos Conference. The metaphor and description is used with permission.

19. Quoted from Frank B. Linderman, *Plenty-Coups: Chief of the Crows* (Lincoln: University of Nebraska Press, 1962), 308–309. Quoted in Jonathan Lear, *Radical Hope: Ethics in the Face of Cultural Devastation* (Cambridge, MA: Harvard University Press, 2006), 2.

20. Lear, *Radical Hope*, 2.

embeddedness, on humility and a much smaller scope of vision than that previously assumed. They all share a focus on hope—hope that starts in infinite particularity, hope that *is what it is* and does not need to feed some larger knowable totality of hope.

What Hall, Leddy, and Lear describe imagistically in terms of the shift from grand narratives of hope to more tentative, humble, trust-based narratives is reflected in the methodological shift taking place within disciplines across the academy and in public discourse. The common response to the breakdown of metanarratives is to develop more local, embedded, particular narratives that invite difference and plurality of meanings and take seriously the diversities of social context, experience, relationships, and so on. A central theological assumption of this methodological shift presupposes that as humans, embedded in creation, we cannot have (nor do we need) access to a "big picture" narrative of human life and history. Rather, this shift intimates that it is in the smaller narratives—the stories of communities, families, and individuals—that possibilities of transcendence, of otherness meeting otherness, are revealed in all sorts of veiled particularity. Indeed, the narratives within which we live are important, for they shape our sense of identity, purpose, and meaning in life. The methodological shift is to more porous, dialogical narrative possibilities that open to otherness and difference and to the unexpected possibility of transcendence.

In terms of hope, implicit in this methodological shift is the affirmation that the end of modernity's metanarrative of hope does not mean that hope ceases to exist. Indeed, people of faith affirm that hope has a transcendent source that will ultimately defy totalizing attempts to master it, even stories of its end. Instead, the end of this metanarrative invites us to dig deeply into multiple narratives that reflect hope's diverse and dynamic presence and movement in life —present and past, in stories of human experience, in theology and the social sciences, and in sacred texts. It is in recovering smaller, more local and multiple narratives that the contours of hope can emerge as complexity that defies all totalizing attempts. Such complexity, ambiguity, and even contradiction together point beyond to a transcendent source of hope that cannot be mastered or narrated by human agency but nonetheless can be recognized in stories of human lives.

The multiplicity of meanings present in understandings of hope in the pastoral and practical theological literature, outlined in chapter 2, point to the multivalence of hope and the extent to which hope becomes possible and present in lived experience in ways that defy all attempts to delimit and circumscribe it. Further, the narratives of hope outlined in chapters 3 through 7 present concrete and, at times, conflicting ways hope is experienced in life. By inductively focusing on very particular narratives of hope in the face of endings and crises, this book responds to the crisis of hope in modernity, suggests of a way forward for research and writing on hope, and also seeks to inspire readers to interrogate their own narratives for hope's presence in unexpected moments and situations.

2

Finding Our Way to Hope
The Possibilities of Multivalence

with Helen Cheung[1]

For in hope we were saved. Now hope that is seen is not hope. For who hopes for what is seen? But if we hope for what we do not see, we wait for it with patience.
Rom. 8:24-25

Hope is no other than the expectation of those things which faith has believed to be truly promised by God. Thus faith believes the veracity of God, hope expects the manifestation of it in due time . . . faith is the foundation on which hope rests, hope nourishes and sustains faith.
John Calvin[2]

When speaking of hope, I am addressing the configuration of cognitive and affective responses to life that believes the future is filled with possibilities and offers a blessing.
Andrew D. Lester[3]

1. The second author of this chapter, Helen Cheung, serves as a manager in mental health services with Houselink Community Homes in Toronto ON. Permission has been generously granted to use material from our chapter "Re-imaging Hope in the Care of Souls: A Literature Review Redefining Hope," *Psychotherapy and the Cure of the Souls,* eds. Thomas St. James O'Connor, Kristine Lund, Patricia Berendsen (Waterloo, ON: Waterloo Lutheran Seminary, 2014), 147-171.

2. John Calvin, *The Institutes of the Christian Religion*, Vol. 1, trans. Ford Lewis Battles (Philadelphia: Westminster, 1960), 506.

3. Andrew D. Lester, *Hope in Pastoral Care and Counseling*, (Louisville: Westminster John Knox, 1995), 62.

Hope is the sum of perceived capabilities to produce routes to desired goals, along with the perceived motivation to use these routes.
C. Richard Snyder[4]

[Hope is] the enduring belief in the attainability of fervent wishes, in spite of dark urges and rages that mark the beginning of existence.
Erik Erikson[5]

Hoping is the perception that what is wanted will happen. It is fueled by desire and occurs in response to felt deprivation.
Donald Capps[6]

Over the last forty years across the fields of health care research, pastoral theology, psychology, systematic theology, and to a certain degree philosophy, there has been growing interest in hope and the importance of hope for fullness of being. Key thinkers from the 1960s to the 1980s challenged those in caregiving disciplines to examine more fully the possibilities for faith-based understandings of hope to enrich care practices and research.[7] As well, the emergence of positive psychology as its own area in psychology in the 1990s meant that, rather than focusing on disease and illness, many psychologists began to focus their efforts on understanding better the dynamics that nourish human flourishing and on examining hope as a key element of well-being. Over these last few decades, as research on hope has expanded exponentially, more and more studies have demonstrated the importance of hope for improving health outcomes.[8] How persons live with or without hope makes a major difference not only to their experience of life and that of their loved ones,

---

4. C. Richard Snyder, *Handbook of Hope: Theory, Measures and Applications*, (Waltham, MA: Academic, 2000), 8.

5. Erik Erikson, Quoted in Donald Capps, *Agents of Hope: A Pastoral Psychology*, (Minneapolis: Fortress Press, 1995), 30.

6. Capps, *Agents of Hope*, 77.

7. See Karl Menninger, "Hope," *American Journal of Psychiatry* 116 (1959): 481–91; Gabriel Marcel, *Homo Viator: Introduction to the Metaphysic of Hope* (South Bend, IN: St. Augustine's, 2010); Robert L. Carrigan, "Where Has Hope Gone? Toward an Understanding of Hope in Pastoral Care," *Pastoral Psychology* 25, no. 1 (1976): 39–53; William F. Lynch, *Images of Hope: Imagination as Healer of the Hopeless* (Notre Dame, IN: University of Notre Dame Press, 1974); Paul W. Pruyser, "Phenomenology and the Dynamics of Hoping," *Journal for the Scientific Study of Religion* 3, no. 1 (1963): 86–96. See also Pruyser, "Maintaining Hope in Adversity," *Pastoral Psychology* 35, no. 2 (1986): 120–31.

8. Martha H. Stoner, "Measuring Hope," in *Instruments for Clinical Health-Care Research*, 3rd ed., ed. Marilyn Frank-Stromborg and Sharon J. Olsen (Mississauga, ON: Jones and Bartlett, 2004), 224.

but also to their experience of pain, recovery, and well-being. Practitioners in many fields agree that a central aspect of care is the nurturing of hope in those for whom one cares.[9] In terms of practical and pastoral theology, hope has been widely accepted as the primary focus for working with individuals, families, communities, and congregations in all the pastoral functions.

The vast and quickly expanding interest in hope might suggest that researchers mostly agree on what hope actually is, but in fact, across the care-centered literature, there is a baffling array of definitions of hope.[10] While all people tend to have their own experiences of hope from which to draw, and while the general population is easily able to engage in discussions about hope, in the literature there is no agreed-upon definition or understanding of exactly what it is we are talking about. This confusion inspired us to conduct a review of the literature, including an inductive analysis, in order to gain a better sense of the central axes and distinctions around which understandings of hope revolve. Our literature review began as a systematic review of the English-language articles in practical and pastoral theology during the thirty-five years between 1976 and 2011 that focus on the presence of hope in human life, in contexts of illness and adversity, and in practices of care.[11] Three databases were searched for articles in practical and pastoral theology that identify hope as a subject and/or keyword. After deletion of duplicates and articles that did not directly address hope in practical or pastoral theology, forty-two articles remained. Both researchers reviewed these articles and independently identified themes emerging from the forty-two articles. Upon discussion, agreement was reached on six dominant themes. To verify and further understand the axes of dialogue implicit in these themes, articles and books that were repeatedly cited in the initial forty-two articles were reviewed, as well as key texts in pastoral and practical theology pertaining to our theme. In the end, the review included fifty-five articles and thirty books from several disciplines, including psychology, health care disciplines, philosophy, and systematic, biblical, practical, and pastoral theology.

---

9. Ibid. See also Capps, *Agents of Hope*; Lester, *Hope in Pastoral Care and Counseling*; see literature also on the Recovery Model, including Barbara Everett, Barb Adams, Jean Johnson, George Kurzawa, Marion Quigley, and Marion Wright, "Recovery Rediscovered: Implications for the Ontario Mental Health System," policy paper, Canadian Mental Health Association, Ontario, March 11, 2003, available at http://ontario.cmha.ca/public_policy/recovery-rediscovered/#.UrDXOyeK4ls.

10. Care-centered literature here includes pastoral theology, spiritual care and counseling, pastoral psychotherapy, psychology, and health care literature.

11. The search was undertaken in the following three databases: ATLA, Proquest Religion, and Religion and Theological Abstracts.

In fleshing out these six axes of hope, we seek to develop a greater understanding of the multivalent dynamics embedded in common experiences of hope. We are in agreement with several other thinkers who consider that hope is a phenomenon that cannot and must not be too easily categorized by means of a rigid definition. Because such a definition could only be formulated if some data were ignored, it would inevitably limit and circumscribe the imaginative possibilities embedded in the very understanding and experience of hope itself. By intentionally shaping this discussion to move toward an open-ended descriptive definition of hope, we seek instead to listen to the data and to develop further a lens for recognizing the multivalence of hope that mysteriously finds its way into human life from all sorts of different experiences, angles, and perspectives.

The following six themes can be described in many ways, and they conflict, intersect, and overlap with each other in many ways, but they do represent the central axes of hope emergent in the literature. The six themes are the origin of hope; the object of hope; hope and agency; hope, optimism, and despair; hope and temporality; and hope in relationship. As we explore these six themes in the discussion that follows, we will elaborate upon the tensions and distinctions exhibited in the literature, which for each theme are best presented in three subparts.

Origin of Hope

What is the source, ground, and origin of hope? How does hope exist? What feeds and nourishes hope? Across the literature, there is a wide range of perspectives regarding the source of hope. Some consider that hope is fundamentally an innate human capacity embedded in the fabric of what it means to be human. Others view the source of hope dialectically. They share the belief that hope includes both the human and the transcendent, the finite and the infinite, the one and the all, the inner and the outer, but they differ about the extent to which the human capacity to hope relates to a larger transcendent source or origin of hope. Still others consider that hope is not a human capacity at all but resides exclusively in transcendent Presence and Being impinging itself within creaturely life.

Hope as an Innate Human Capacity

Many of those who consider hope to be an innate human capacity are pastoral theologians, psychologists, and care practitioners influenced largely by the human potential movement and by positive psychology.[12] Donald Capps, following Erik Erikson, argues that hope finds its origin as an innate capacity that can be brought forward in relationship with a caregiver.[13] He describes hope as "an attitude or disposition that exists as an integral part of ourselves."[14] Hope is something with which humans are born, something that is present in all and that needs to be nourished throughout life. It persists in the human even when there is no obvious ground for it.[15] Capps makes a close link between autonomy and hope.[16] Some consider that hope exists as an inner human capacity that enables life, so that when hope dies in a person, physical death is not far off.[17] Snyder argues that people range from high-hope to low-hope persons. His theory suggests that, one way or another, hope is part of the makeup of humans, whether in high or low levels.[18] Social psychologist Ezra Stotland, a theorist of hope, considers hope to be an inner motivational force in all people that functions as that which enables humans to act.[19]

HOPE WITHIN AND TRANSCENDENT OF HUMAN CAPACITY

Those thinkers who argue that hope is dialectical, both present within and transcending human capacity, engage the source of hope in a variety of ways.[20]

12. See Capps, *Agents of Hope*; Howard Clinebell, *Counseling for Spiritually Empowered Wholeness: A Hope-Centered Approach* (New York: Haworth, 1995); Gregory C. Ellison II, "Late Stylin' in an Ill-Fitting Suit: Donald Capps' Artistic Approach to the Hopeful Self and Its Implications for Unacknowledged African American Young Men," *Pastoral Psychology* 58 (2009): 477–89; David Lee Jones, "A Pastoral Model for Caring for Persons with Diminished Hope," *Pastoral Psychology* 58 (2009): 641–54; Cameron Lee, "Dispositional Resiliency and Adjustment in Protestant Pastors: A Pilot Study," *Pastoral Psychology* 59 (2010): 631–40; Menninger, "Hope"; Richard C. Snyder, "Hypothesis: There Is Hope," in *Handbook of Hope*, ed. R. C. Snyder (Waltham, MA: Academic, 2000); Ezra Stotland, *The Psychology of Hope* (San Francisco, CA: Jossey-Bass, 1969).

13. Capps, *Agents of Hope*, 31.

14. Ibid., 28.

15. "Hope is a basic [human] strength precisely because it persists even when we have no objective grounds for trust." Capps in discussing Erikson, ibid., 30.

16. Ibid., 28.

17. "Hope is something all people need until their last breath. . . . Life is hope." B. A. Hall, quoted in Stoner, "Measuring Hope," 219.

18. Snyder, *Handbook of Hope*, 13.

19. As described in Stoner, "Measuring Hope," 216.

20. Carrigan, "Where Has Hope Gone?"; Thomas V. Gerkin, *An Introduction to Pastoral Care* (Nashville: Abingdon, 1997); Russell Herbert, *Living Hope* (Werrington, UK: Epworth, 2006); Simon S. M. Kwan, "Interrogating 'Hope': The Pastoral Theology of Hope and Positive Psychology,'" *International Journal of Practical Theology* 14 (2010): 47–67; Lester, *Hope in Pastoral Care and Counseling*; Gabriel Marcel, *Homo Viator*; Neil Pembroke, "Witnessing to Hope in the Christian Community through Irony," *Pastoral Psychology* 58 (2009): 433–43.

Many of them come from or are open to religious worldviews that honor certain ways of thinking about the relationship between the immanent and the transcendent, the one and the Whole, the creature and the Creator, the historical and the eternal.

Some consider that the presence of hope reflects the presence of God in life.[21] Whenever one hopes, the divine a priori is intimated. Russell Herbert weaves his understanding of the innate capacity to hope with a theological anthropology. For Herbert, the human capacity to hope is intrinsically related to an inner yearning toward God, inspired and drawn forth by the movement of God within and beyond the self: "A [pastoral] theology that recognizes hope as a basic component of human nature and as something that reflects the innate God-ward orientation that is woven into the fabric of life itself is a theology that believes that at least the potential for hope resides in all people."[22]

Philosopher Gabriel Marcel, whose work on hope has been influential for many across different fields, holds that the inner yearning or hope must be met outside the self in an encounter with outer dimensions of being, communal and transcendent. For both Marcel and theologian William Lynch, hope is an interior sense that needs response from outside and has meaning only as it relates to a finite or transcendent other as an act of collaboration.[23]

Some posit that ultimately human "hope should be grounded on God's promise, not human possibilities."[24] As such, the human capacity to hope is completely related to a reliance on God's ultimate mercy. Trusting in God's promises is a key component of hope.[25] God's promises in some sense function as both the source and object of hope.

HOPE TRANSCENDS THE HUMAN

The final category includes several thinkers who argue for the transcendent origin of hope.[26] These thinkers generally represent theistic religious

21. Pruyser, "Maintaining Hope," *Pastoral Psychology*, 120–30.

22. Herbert, *Living Hope*, 92. "Hoping for resurrection . . . means hoping for hope itself, because only resurrection hope can provide a sufficiently robust basis for all other hopes."

23. See Stoner's description of Marcel and Lynch in "Measuring Hope," 215.

24. Kwan, "Interrogating 'Hope,'" 63. Kwan argues that the contributions of positive psychology to pastoral theological notions of hope are important and helpful for practice; he urges a more dialectical intersection between theology and psychology with a privileging of theological understandings of the ground of being.

25. It is important to note that here hope is about trusting in God's promises, which distinguishes it from trusting in God (next section).

26. Kirk A. Bingaman, "A Pastoral Theological Approach to the New Anxiety," *Pastoral Psychology* 59 (2010): 659–70; Cynthia Bourgeault, *Mystical Hope: Trusting in the Mercy of God* (Lanham, MD: Cloister,

perspectives but differ on how divine presence is or is not related to lived human experience. Grenz critiques the idea that the source of hope is found in human capacity. He argues against the anthropological starting point and foundationalism inherent in this idea, along with the way in which it essentializes hope as a human attribute. In general, he is critical of pastoral theologians' appeal to modern psychology rather than theology for understanding hope.[27] He argues that true Christian hope must be pessimistic about the inherent potential of the human. Instead, the sources of hope are the sure and certain promises narrated in the Scriptures, which place the horizon of hope in God's promise for the consummation of all things.[28]

Others envision a participatory relationship wherein the acts of human hoping participate in the divine presence in life. Julie Neraas calls this theistic hope wherein "the ultimate locus of hope is in God and God alone. . . . Hope is a dimension of the divine that we share in."[29] "Ultimately, hope is divine energy and intelligence moving toward the accomplishment of its purposes: it makes use of us rather than we of it."[30] Michael Whelan holds that "the source of hope is beyond the person, beyond the moment, beyond material circumstances. Hope-filled people know in their bones that their story is part of . . . a cosmic story that is, in turn, part of an eternal story."[31]

Ralph Underwood and Andrew Root both identify themselves with theologians of the cross, paradoxically identifying the hiddenness of God as the only ground of hope.[32] Root urges contemporary Christian pastoral theologians

2001); Carrigan, "Where Has Hope Gone?"; Stanley J. Grenz, "The Hopeful Pessimist," *Journal of Pastoral Care* 54 (2000): 297–322; Stephen T. Hall, "A Working Theology of Prison Ministry," *Journal of Pastoral Care and Counseling* 58, no. 3 (2004): 169–78; Daniel J. Louw, "Pastoral Care and the Therapeutic Dimension of Christian Hope," *Pastoral Sciences* 17 (1998): 81–96; Louw, "The HIV Pandemic from the Perspective of a *Theologia Resurrectionis*: Resurrection Hope as a Pastoral Critique on the Punishment and Stigma Paradigm," *Journal of Theology for Southern Africa* 126 (2006): 100–114; Julie E. Neraas, *Apprenticed to Hope: A Sourcebook for Difficult Times* (Minneapolis: Fortress Press, 2009); Andrew Root, "A Theology of the Cross and Ministry in Our Time," *Dialog* 48, no. 2 (2009): 187–93; Ralph L. Underwood, "Enlarging Hope for Wholeness: Ministry with Persons in Pain," *Journal of Pastoral Care and Counseling* 60, no. 1 (2006): 3–12; Michael Whelan, "The Human Ground of Hope: A Pastoral Reflection," *Australasian Catholic Record* 82, no. 4 (October 2005): 454–63.

27. Grenz, "Hopeful Pessimist," 306–307.

28. Ibid., 308. It is helpful to note too that Simon Kwan, drawing on Stephen Pattinson and Don Browning, cautions against using psychology as a starting point or primary reference point for pastoral theology, rather than the rich traditions of theology. See Kwan, "Interrogating 'Hope,'" 48, 66.

29. Neraas, *Apprenticed to Hope*, 132.

30. Bourgeault, *Mystical Hope*, 79.

31. Whelan, "The Human Ground of Hope."

to fully enter the nihilism of the present time, for it is here in the fullness of suffering that hope meets us: "God is present right in the middle of the nihilism of despair. . . . It is in suffering, hiddenness, and opposites that God is found."[33] With Luther, Root suggests that we must not trust in but rather despair of the capacity of the human as a ground for hope. Such despair is the beginning of true hope. Paradoxically, it is in the failure of human capacity that we encounter hope in the beaten and weak person of Jesus Christ. In Jesus, the hidden promise of resurrection, the hidden promise of hope, is unexpectedly present.[34] Thus, hope's origin and source is hidden in divine presence when human capacity has reached its end.

OBJECT OF HOPE

Closely related to questions about the source and origin of hope are questions about the object of hope. In some instances, these two themes interweave to such an extent that it is difficult to distinguish them. However, in the literature, much attention is given to the object of hope. The biggest area of tension revolves around whether hope requires future outcomes or goals as its object or whether the object of hope is more open-ended. Between those who hold these two perspectives lie many who consider that both goal achievement and open-ended trust are important elements of hope. In the literature, this distinction is often explored through the categories of *hopes* and *hope*. Hopes are desired goals or outcomes located in the future. Hope, in contrast, is a larger, more transcendent notion, not tied to outcomes or goals but rather manifested in a way of being open, trusting, or expectant. In some cases, this larger, open-ended hope is related directly to God as the object of hope.

HOPE'S OBJECT AS DESIRED GOALS AND OUTCOMES

Not surprisingly, it is primarily the writers representing and influenced by positive psychology who closely relate hope to achievement of desired goals.[35]

32. Ralph L. Underwood, "Hope in the Face of Chronic Pain and Mortality ," *Pastoral Psychology* 58 (2009): 662.

33. Andrew Root, "The Theology of the Cross and Ministry in Our Time," *Dialog* 48, no. 2 (2009): 191.

34. Ibid., 192.

35. Capps, *Agents of Hope*; Verna Carson, Karen Soeken, and Patricia Grimm, "Hope and Its Relationship to Spiritual Well-Being," *Journal of Psychology and Theology* 16, no. 2 (1988): 159–67; Clinebell, *Counseling for Spiritually Empowered Wholeness*; Ellison II, "Late Stylin'"; D. Jones, "A Pastoral Model"; Kaye Herth, "Abbreviated Instrument to Measure Hope: Development and Psychometric

They privilege hopes over hope—some to such a degree that hopes constitute the sum total of hope in human life.[36] Snyder and associates convincingly argue that hope is directly related to developing pathways to achieve desired goals. This theory of hope easily gives itself to care practices common in health care today.[37] Clients work with caregivers to create achievable and desired goals and then to develop means to achieve those goals. It has been well demonstrated that this understanding of hope is embedded in the counseling practices of brief solution-focused therapy and those influenced by the human potential movement.[38] Further, there are several examples of pastoral theologians building directly on Snyder's work in their research and practice.[39]

In Capps's work on hope in pastoral practice and in his basic definition of hoping itself, it is clear that he emphasizes the achievement of desired outcomes in the experience of hope.[40] The focus is on realizable hopes that are projected into the future and draw a person toward that future. An important element in Capps's understanding is that the future goals are *desired* goals. Future goals are hopes, latent with positive connotation. It is inaccurate to say that Capps considers hopes to be the absolute sum total of hope. However, in his work, he focuses almost exclusively on the ways that hopes manifest hope in pastoral practice and does not elaborate on larger notions of hope.

HOPE'S OBJECT AS GOALS AND OPEN-ENDEDNESS

The second set of thinkers, although they engage the topic of hope dialectically in varying ways, all privilege hope over hopes—that is, open-ended or existential hope over goal-focused hopes.[41] Among those with this view, the

Evaluation," *Journal of Advanced Nursing* 17, no. 10 (1992): 1251–1259; Lee, "Dispositional Resiliency"; M. L. Nowotny, "Assessment of Hope in Patients with Cancer: Development of an Instrument," *Oncology Nursing Forum* 16, no. 1 (1989): 57–61; Natalie Pattison and Christopher Lee, "Hope against Hope in Cancer at the End of Life," *Journal of Religion and Health* 50 (2011): 731–42; Snyder, *Handbook of Hope*; Stotland, *The Psychology of Hope*.

36. Stoner, "Measuring Hope," 216. Stoner quotes Ezra Stotland: "Hope is the perceived probability of success in obtaining a goal."

37. See especially C. R. Snyder's work, *Handbook on Hope*.

38. Kwan, "Interrogating 'Hope,'" 49–51.

39. Lee," Dispositional Resiliency," 633: "Hope is a cognitive process that has the ability to see many routes (pathways) to reach future goals and the capacity to reach goals." See also Carson et al., "Hope and Its Relationship to Spiritual Well-Being," 159–67.

40. "Hoping "is the perception that what one wants to happen will happen, a perception that is fueled by desire and a response to felt deprivation. Hopes envision the realizable." Capps, *Agents of Hope*, 77.

41. Megory Anderson, "Spiritual Journey with the Dying, Liminality, and the Nature of Hope," *Liturgy* 22, no. 3 (2007): 41–47; Carrigan, "Where Has Hope Gone?"; Karin Dufault and Benita

extent to which hopes and hope are connected varies, as does the extent to which the larger notions of hope are related to a transcendent being or to a generalized trust in the universe as a basis of hope. Several researchers and thinkers in this grouping warn that inversion of hopes and hope—or the assumption that individual goal achievement can bear the weight of existential hope—can lead to despair and hopelessness, and undermine both hope and hopes.

Andrew Lester's categories well illustrate this perspective.[42] He uses the terms *finite* and *transfinite hope* to highlight the importance of the link between finite hope invested by finite creatures in finite objects, desires, and processes[43] and transfinite hope "that is placed in subjects and processes that go beyond physiological sensing and the material world."[44] Finite hope is but penultimate: it depends in some sense on transfinite hope. In his discussion on transfinite hope, Lester draws on Marcel, arguing that "hope . . . tends inevitably to transcend the particular objects to which it at first seems to be attached. . . . Transfinite hope embraces the mystery and excitement of open-ended future and the not-yet."[45] Like others, including Marcel, Lester argues that the relationship between transfinite and finite hope is important because transfinite hope undergirds and informs finite hopes.[46] While Lester does not insist that transfinite hope inevitably manifests faith in a transcendent presence, others consider that goal achievement in this life (hopes achieved) functions as a foretaste or a prelude to the promised eschatological future in God (or transfinite hope).[47]

Martocchio, "Hope: Its Spheres and Dimensions," *Nursing Clinic of North America* 20 (1985): 379–91; Gerkin, *An Introduction to Pastoral Care*; Herbert, *Living Hope*; Kwan, "Interrogating 'Hope'"; Lester, *Hope in Pastoral Care and Counseling*; Marcel, *Homo Viator*; Richard Meyer, "Integrating Cognitive Theory and Theology," *American Journal of Pastoral Counseling* 2, no. 4 (2000): 3–29; Pattison and Lee, "Hope against Hope"; Pembroke, "Witnessing to Hope"; Robert L. Richardson, "Where There Is Hope, There Is Life: Toward a Biology of Hope," *Journal of Pastoral Care* 54, no. 1 (2000): 75–83; Howard Stone and Andrew Lester, "Hope and Possibility: Envisioning the Future in Pastoral Conversation," *Journal of Pastoral Care* 55, no. 3 (2001): 259–69.

42. Pattison and Lee include both understandings of hope. Hope is (1) tangible and practical outcomes; (2) goals and actions; (3) emotional support; and (4) peace and meaning. Pattison and Lee, "Hope against Hope," 739–40.

43. Lester, *Hope in Pastoral Care*, 63.

44. Ibid., 64.

45. Ibid., 65.

46. Ibid., 66.

47. Kwan, "Interrogating 'Hope,'" 64.

Similar to Lester's distinctions, the oft-cited health care research of Karin Dufault and Benita Martocchio shows the importance of these overlapping and intersecting understandings of the object of hope/hopes. Dufault and Martocchio use the term *particularized hope* to refer to specific hopes and goals and *generalized hope* to refer to a broader spirit of trust in the face of open-ended possibility.[48] Again, generalized hope is held up to be a basis upon which particularized hope emerges. At the same time, particularized hope can feed a larger sense of generalized hope or hopefulness.[49] In an early nursing study on hope, Stanley includes both "expectation of significant future outcome" and "having a quality of transcendence" in the elements central to hope.[50]

HOPE'S OBJECT AS OPEN-ENDED

Several thinkers and researchers challenge the idea that individual goal-focused hopes have any place in understandings of hope at all.[51] Pruyser, for example, writes, "True hope is not goal-oriented. Hoping does not deal with objects at all but focuses on global or existential conditions: one hopes to be liberated when in captivity, to be healed when sick, to be blessed when feeling damned . . . , or to see the light at the end of the tunnel when in darkness."[52] Following Pruyser and Marcel, many consider that true hope "cannot have specific goals because the final stage . . . always remains open. Having specific goals means closing off the possibility of novelty and taking present knowledge to be final."[53] Hoping is process oriented, not goals oriented. Pruyser sees goal orientation more as wishing, while a process-oriented way of being is akin to hope.[54]

48. Particularized hope is "self-confident expectation of specific future goals or personally significant future good for the self." Generalized hope is "a generalized sense of the future." Stoner, "Measuring Hope," 218.

49. Ibid., 217. Also see Herth, "Abbreviated Instrument to Measure Hope." See also Nowotny, "Assessment of Hope," 57–61.

50. Stoner, "Measuring Hope," 217.

51. Bourgeault, *Mystical Hope*; Carrigan, "Where Has Hope Gone?"; Grenz, "Hopeful Pessimist"; Herbert, *Living Hope*; Kwan, "Interrogating 'Hope'"; Ryan LaMothe, "Reflections on Pastoral Leadership in the Face of Cultural Communal 'Ruin,'" *Journal of Pastoral Theology* 20, no. 1 (2010): 10–21; Louw, "Pastoral Care and the Therapeutic Dimension of Christian Hope"; Louw, "Creative Hope and Imagination in a Practical Theology of Aesthetic (Artistic) Reason," *Religion and Theology* 8, nos. 3–4 (2001): 327–44; Louw, "The HIV Pandemic"; Marcel, *Homo Viator*; Neraas, *Apprenticed to Hope*; Pruyser, "Phenomenology and the Dynamics of Hoping"; Root, "A Theology of the Cross"; Glenn D. Weaver, "Senile Dementia and a Resurrection Theology," *Theology Today* 42 (1986): 444–56; Whelan, "The Human Ground of Hope, 454–63.

52. Pruyser, "Maintaining Hope," 121.

53. Kwan, "Interrogating Hope," 63; Pruyser, "Maintaining Hope," 126.

Grenz draws on Daniel Louw's distinction that identifies the object of our hope not as the future, but rather as the God of the future with whom we exist in relationship:[55] "In the end, the final object of hope is not the future itself, but the God of the future."[56] While it appears that there is a specific object of hope in God, God exists in freedom so there is an unknowable dynamism that cannot be nailed down in any specific way. Such hope requires living in a posture of trust in the one who brings forth resurrection from death, who inverts our expectations in the hidden possibilities of death and life.[57]

In the health care literature, too, we find such open-ended notions of hope without reference to specific hopes or goals. "Hope is a complex phenomenon involving the variables of love, mutuality, freedom, and newness communicated through a positive orientation."[58] In work on hope done by a Buddhist researcher, there is a similar critique of a goals or outcome orientation of hope. Instead, hope is considered to be radical consent to what is and what will be in a spirit of openness.[59]

HOPE AND AGENCY

The role of agency in the construction of hope raises many questions for people serving in practices of care. Indeed, this theme is closely related to the themes of the origin of hope and the object of hope just discussed. However, different nuances emerge when we look at hope from this angle. Is hope primarily about the willful enacting of human agency, about making things happen as we want them to happen? Is it primarily about divine action and agency and the human waiting upon such action? Is it about the dialectical intersection between human and divine agency? Or finally, is it less about active doing and agency and more about being, letting go and trusting what is?

54. Similarly, Maynard describes that hope is related closely to love: "Hope may be found in self-giving love that transcends death. The fruit of hope in the face of traumatic death is resurrection life, a life of justice empowered by dangerous memories of love to which survivors testify." Jane F. Maynard, *Transfiguring Loss: Julian of Norwich as a Guide for Survivors of Traumatic Grief* (Cleveland: Pilgrim, 2006), 10.

55. Grenz, "Hopeful Pessimist," 309. Grenz draws from Daniel Louw, "Pastoral Care and the Therapeutic Dimension of Christian Hope," 82.

56. Grenz, "Hopeful Pessimist," 308–309.

57. See also Andrew Root, "Hope through Death," in *The Promise of Despair* (Nashville: Abingdon, 2010), 139–50.

58. See Thompson study in Stoner, "Measuring Hope," 217.

59. Kanae Kinoshita, "For a Buddhist Chaplain in a Multi-faith Setting: Is There a Place for Hope for People Who Are Dying?" (MA diss., University of Sunderland, 2007).

HOPE AND HUMAN AGENCY: WILLING AND ACTING

Several researchers and thinkers consider that hope revolves around the full flourishing of human agency.[60] The desire for change is interpreted to be that which propels the human will to act with drive and creativity toward a better future. The focus is on active doing through the power of the will. Here, one's agential will drives one toward a desired future fulfillment initiated from felt deprivation. Capps well represents this perspective. Drawing on Erikson, he ties hope closely to autonomy and the enacting of the autonomous individual upon circumstance: "Our explorations into the origins of hope in infancy and early childhood . . . enable us to see that autonomy and hope go together."[61] While Capps and some others in this group do suggest that both human and divine agency are central to pastoral counseling and care, Capps does not elaborate on the role of divine agency in his discussion of counseling strategies.

Snyder, in his research on hope, emphasizes the centrality of human agency in relationship to the goal and the pathway to the goal. When failure of the expected pathway to the goal produces hopelessness, the role of agency is either to imagine new pathways or to reset goals so that they are attainable.[62] The implication is that without active human agency, hope is impossible. Hope arises when a person projects herself or himself into the future, compares this projection with the present, and is empowered to make decisions to change the present so as to move it closer to the projected future. In this instance, hope is about embracing the role of the self in forming the future.[63] Human agency, with its eyes fixed on a goal, can change the world, make a difference, and construct a beautiful future.[64]

For many in counseling, psychology, social work, ministry, and spiritual care working with clients to help build a sense of agency is central to good practice. The focus of care is to enhance the client's sense of agency and empowerment to change present conditions.[65] The human will is turned in a certain direction, and the pathway to get from the present to the desired future is broken down into achievable parts. Anyone in caregiving professions knows

---

60. Capps, *Agents of Hope*; Herth, "Abbreviated Instrument"; Lee, "Dispositional Resiliency"; Lester, *Hope in Pastoral Care and Counseling*; Nowotny, "Assessment of Hope"; Snyder, *Handbook of Hope*; Stone and Lester, "Hope and Possibility."

61. Capps, *Agents of Hope*, 28. Even in his title, *Agents of Hope*, Capps links the centrality of human agency with hope.

62. Snyder, *Handbook of Hope*, 10–13.

63. Kwan, "Interrogating 'Hope,'" 53.

64. Ibid., 52.

65. Ibid., 57. See also Stoner, "Measuring Hope," 216.

that such care can be highly effective with many different clients and situations. At the same time, it is clear that focus on the human will and agency does not by any means exhaust hope's possibilities.

HOPE AND DIVINE AGENCY: WAITING AND RECEPTIVITY

A second perspective on hope and agency locates agency primarily in divine action.[66] Hope, therefore, exists in part through the practice of waiting on God. In the Hebrew Scriptures, priority is placed on God's agency as the basis of hope.[67] John Swinton emphasizes the agency of God over human agency: "Christians wait in hope for the day when that re-creating work will be completed. Despite the presence of evil and suffering, the world is being shaped by God."[68] Neraas, in her reflections on hope, retrieves an understanding of hope from the Hebrew Scriptures that highlights the extent to which divine and human agencies are bound together as the defining story of Jewish biblical history.[69] The interaction of divine agency and human agency is central to hope, and there is a lively, dialogical quality about it.

In referring to Jürgen Moltmann's theology of hope, Simon Kwan notes that "authentic Christian hope is not based on things that human activities can fulfill. To the contrary, whatever positive changes we attain will become disappointing because, in the end, everyone dies and returns to nothing. Hope should be grounded on God's promise, not human possibilities . . . . If Christian faith grounds hope in God's promise, then what makes people move forward

66. Bingaman, "The New Anxiety"; Carrigan, "Where Has Hope Gone?"; Grenz, "Hopeful Pessimist"; Kwan, "Interrogating 'Hope'"; Hall, "A Working Theology of Prison Ministry"; Louw, "Pastoral Care and the Therapeutic Dimensions of Christian Hope"; Louw, "The HIV Pandemic"; John Manoussakis, "The Anarchic Principle of Christian Eschatology in the Eucharistic Tradition of the Eastern Church," *Harvard Theological Review* 100, no. 1 (2007): 29–46; Meyer, "Integrating Cognitive Theory"; Ralph Underwood, "Personal and Professional Integrity in Relation to Pastoral Assessment," *Pastoral Psychology* 31, no. 2 (1982): 109–117; Whelan, "Human Ground of Hope."

67. See Pamela R. McCarroll, *Waiting at the Foot of the Cross: Toward a Theology of Hope* (Eugene OR: Pickwick, 2014), 194. For example, the words translated as 'hope for' into English from the Hebrew, can most often also be translated as 'wait for.' Hope is understood as waiting expectantly, looking out for, yearning for, persevering and trusting in God, the one who acts to bring salvation and wholeness. The grammatical structure of the Hebrew language suggests that the one who hopes or waits is shaped by that for which one hopes and waits. Ultimately, the worthy object of hope is God and God's action in history. Human agency is important only insofar as it correlates to God's action and agency. Thus, hope is reflected in receptivity and waiting upon divine agency and action in history while also including aspects of continuity and discontinuity between the action of creature and creator.

68. John Swinton, *Raging with Compassion: Pastoral Responses to the Problem of Evil* (Grand Rapids: Eerdmans, 2007), 52.

69. Neraas, *Apprenticed to Hope*, 139.

fearlessly is not our own agency, but God's. What keeps things open to the future is not our willpower, but God's."[70] Similarly, Grenz's article emphasizes pessimism about human agency and what humans might do. His understanding of hope focuses solely on what God will do: bringing forth life from death, saying no to evil and yes to creation.[71] Both the human relationship to God and God's own active agency are the center of hope. Human agents cannot presume to know and recognize God's agency. Rather, God's agency and will are ultimate and must be waited upon prayerfully.

The focus on divine agency can lead in a number of directions. However, what is central is the embedded theology of such an idea. Just as the anthropological focus on agency suggests that humans exist primarily as beings who "will," so the suggestion here can be that God as active agent exists primarily as one who wills. God's willing may be considered to be manifested in God's power to control and make things happen. Such a perspective is common to parts of mainline Christianity, much of Islam, and parts of Judaism. In these belief structures and in the secular version of the same idea articulated in the phrase "it was meant to be," the suggestion is that whatever happens is God's will and was meant to happen. In this case, hope is primarily about waiting—obedience to and acceptance of God's (or the universe's) agency and will. One is to wait and trust that, even if one does not like what is happening, hope resides in consenting and persevering, knowing that a transcendent will prevails and that it is ultimately for the good.

In contrast, some hold that God's agency is shaped, embodied, and communicated in love and that our call is to participate in this love. Thus, consent to love's way in the world, bringing oneself into alignment with love, is the way of hope and feeds hope. The possibility for connection between creature and Creator exists in the presence of love in the world. God is love. Therefore, when one participates in loving relations and actions in the world, God's will and agency are being enacted. The expression of human love in the world is discerned, however imperfectly, as an expression of God's active agency in the world. Carrigan suggests that "hope, in the Christian sense, is living by grace." Hope trusts in God's love rather than prescribing what God will do.[72] The emphasis is on the activity and assurance of God's love as priority. In this case, love constitutes the manifestation of God's agency.

---

70. Kwan, "Interrogating 'Hope,'" 63–64.

71. Grenz, "Hopeful Pessimist," 310.

72. Carrigan, "Where Has Hope Gone?," 48.

No Agency: Being and Trusting

Still others consider that the focus on human or divine agency willing and doing is a problematic way for understanding hope. Rather, hope is considered to be more about trust and receptivity than about active agency, more about being than doing; more about a process than a goal.[73] From this point of view, human agency and willing are relativized by an emphasis on process, being, and trusting, while at the same time neither God nor the universe is seen primarily as an active, doing, and willing agent.

Pruyser agrees with Gabriel Marcel's understanding that hoping involves a process rather than a goal: "The self is not a strong action centre; instead hoping involves humility,"[74] and "Hoping is a matter of being, not of having" or wishing or desiring.[75] Whelan similarly rejects the idea of human agency and doing as the focus of hope. Rather, he describes hope as "an expression of existence, a manifestation of a person's very being that emerges when s/he is more or less at one with what is real in and around."[76] Quoting Václav Havel, he goes on to argue that "hope is a state of mind . . . a dimension of the soul, and an orientation of the spirit and the heart."[77]

According to Neil Pembroke, human participation in hope can be best understood by integrating a non-Western concept of *wu wei*, a concept that holds together active and passive ways of being. Pembroke draws on the Taoist tradition to point to a way of being that implies a relativizing of divine and human agency in relation to one another. *Wu wei* implies that one takes action by non-action. One hits the target without taking aim, behaving intuitively. *Wu wei*, Pembroke explains, is an intuitive and spontaneous embrace of the real self.[78] In describing this way of being in his research on depressed individuals, Pembroke says that *wu wei* "invites depressed individuals to return to themselves, to stop analyzing themselves, to stop trying to fix themselves. *Wu wei* invites them to stay right where they are even in the experience of negativity."[79] For Pembroke and others similarly minded, hope is not based on

---

73. Bourgeault, *Mystical Hope*; Carrigan, "Where Has Hope Gone?"; LaMothe, "Reflections on Pastoral Leadership"; Manoussakis, "Anarchic Principle"; Neil Pembroke, *Pastoral Care in Worship* (New York: T&T Clark, 2010); Pruyser, "Maintaining Hope."

74. Pruyser, "Maintaining Hope," 121.

75. Ibid., 128. Louw also queries the idea of human agency in relation to hope. He describes that hope is "a qualitative state of being despite the existing voidness and nothingness"—a state of being that reflects "new being in Christ." Louw, "Pastoral Care and the Therapeutic Dimension of Christian Hope," 82.

76. Whelan, "Human Ground of Hope," 454.

77. Ibid., 460.

78. Pembroke, *Pastoral Care in Worship*, 118.

active human agency but rather is an entrusting of oneself to a larger flow and whole—not so much by an act of the will but rather by an act of restraining the will, of consent to that which is beyond.

Those who align themselves with a theology of the cross consider as suspect all promises of triumphal hope, both in terms of human will and agency and in terms of human perceptions of divine will and agency. While the source and locus of hope is God revealed in the cross of Christ, the human perception of God commonly rests in triumphalism—a perception that in fact takes humans down the wrong path, away from the God revealed most powerfully in the weakness of the cross. Any positive focus on divine will and agency that leans toward triumphalism and glory is suspect, for it presumes to know more of the hiddenness of God than can be discerned by the human mind. God's hidden presence is most near at the end of human agency and willing, when humans are brought to their knees in humility and the helplessness of the will. Hope exists in this hidden God, revealed in the suffering of the cross. Hope, therefore, is most present in the restraining of the human will so as to trust in the one who meets us in all our frailty, failure, and finitude.

HOPE, OPTIMISM, AND DESPAIR

How does hope relate to optimism, and how does it relate to despair or to the negations of life? Is hope about the enacting of an optimistic view of life? Is it about fueling desire that is precipitated by deprivation? Does hope emerge in dialogue with despair as a dynamic interaction taking place within human souls? Is despair somehow the beginning of hope, the point at which emerges the paradox of the impossible becoming possible? Or is hope a category that resists the binary poles of optimism and despair and that instead can include both or neither of these categories in different ways and levels? Throughout the literature, it is common for thinkers and researchers to discuss distinctions and overlapping relationships between hope, optimism, and despair. The various ways in which these distinctions and relationships are understood in the literature have the effect of making the multivalent character of hope even more complex.

HOPE AND OPTIMISM AGAINST DESPAIR

For several theorists, hope is understood as the polar opposite of despair and hopelessness such that the two cannot coexist.[80] Further, hope and optimism

---

79. Ibid., 118. Pembroke quotes Siroj Sorajjakool, "*Wu wei* (Non-Doing) and Negativity of Depression," *Journal of Religion and Health* 39, no. 2 (2000): 165–66.

are deemed to be close companions. Having a positive attitude and thinking optimistically makes all the difference for hope: "Optimism and hope are distinct (though closely related) phenomena."[81] It is perhaps Snyder who most fully represents the perspective of the proximity of hope and optimism and the mutually negating substance of hope with despair. For Snyder, hope is focused on desired goals for the future and developing the appropriate pathways necessary to reach these goals. Over and against pathology-related notions of psychology, wherein the focus is on addressing problems, positive psychology seeks to support human flourishing as an end toward which hope moves. Hope's movement is forward, so to speak, directed toward a future that promises good outcomes.

In Capps's definition of hope, influenced as we have seen by positive psychology, hoping is considered to be "a perception that is fuelled by desire and a response to felt deprivation."[82] The fact that "felt deprivation" fuels the desire for something other than what is indicates that the reaction against this negation is what propels hope forward. For Capps, despair is the chief enemy of hope. As polar opposites, they erode each other and cannot coexist.[83] Similarly, Howard Clinebell, a proponent of the human potential movement, considers hope and hopelessness to be mutually exclusive, binary opposites on a linear trajectory extending in one direction toward hope and in the other to hopelessness/despair.[84] Hope leads to possibility, and hopelessness leads to impossibility.[85] Hope, like optimism, exists in a positive attitude toward life that brings about positive change. Thus, for Clinebell and others, it is essential that the counselor have a hope-centered approach to the client's growth. For Capps, the role of the counselor in working with people who are hopeless is to turn

---

80. Capps, *Agents of Hope*; Herth, "Abbreviated Instrument to Measure Hope"; Lee, "Dispositional Resiliency"; R. F. McGee, "Hope: A Factor Influencing Crisis Resolution," *Journal of Advanced Nursing Science* 6, no. 4 (1984): 34–44; Snyder, *Handbook of Hope*; Underwood, "Personal and Professional Integrity in Relation to Pastoral Assessment."

81. Pembroke, *Pastoral Care in Worship*, 97.

82. Capps, *Agents of Hope*, 53.

83. Kwan, "Interrogating 'Hope,'" 54.

84. "Growth counseling is much more than a set of techniques. It is, at its heart, a basic orientation toward people—a growth- and a hope-centered way of perceiving, experiencing and relating to them. The growth-hope perspective is more essential than any particular technique." Clinebell, *Counseling for Spiritually Empowered Wholeness*, 54.

85. Kwan, "Interrogating 'Hope,'" 50. See also Ralph Underwood, "Enlarging Hope for Wholeness: Ministry with Persons in Pain," *Journal of Pastoral Care and Counseling* 60, nos. 1–2 (2006): 3–12. Underwood uses *hope* interchangeably with *optimism*.

their eyes in a different direction—from the suffering present toward fulfillment in the future, from unrealizable goals to realizable ones.[86]

Within the nursing literature, McGee similarly argues that hope and hopelessness exist on opposite ends of a continuum, so in that sense, they are mutually exclusive. However, while McGee, like Capps and Snyder, sees hope and hopelessness as widely separated poles of a continuum, McGee's approach is more dialectical. The theory argues that the ideal location for humans is to be within the middle range of the continuum wherein hope and hopelessness can interact. This location allows for consent and acceptance of that within life that is hopeless and unchangeable combined with a positive outlook on that which is open and changeable.[87] If one moves too far toward the hopeless pole, one gives in to what is considered to be inevitable. If one moves too far toward the hopeful pole, one can be immobilized by feelings of invulnerability.

HOPE AND DESPAIR IN MUTUAL GENERATIVITY

Among thinkers and researchers in the next grouping, there is commonly a need both to identify the dynamic relationship between hope and despair (or other negations in life such as suffering) and to distinguish hope from optimism.[88] In this perspective, the confusion of hope with optimism is considered false hope, a cooptation of modern Western priorities that undermines hope's existential moorings.[89] For example, Root writes, "Hope is qualitatively different from optimism, because hope bears death; hope seeks a future not by ignoring or denying death (looking on the bright side) but by living through it."[90] Hope and hopelessness exist dialectically and paradoxically in mutual generativity. Hope is impossible without engagement with despair and the negations of life.

Representing this position well, Kwan argues that "hope and hopelessness have a close relationship, being mutually generating and subjugating, instead of excluding each other and never co-existing."[91] Quoting Cornell West, he

---

86. Kwan, "Interrogating 'Hope,'" 54.

87. Stoner, "Measuring Hope," 118.

88. Carrigan, "Where Has Hope Gone?"; Herbert, *Living Hope*; Kwan, "Interrogating 'Hope'"; Ryan LaMothe, "What Hope Is There?," *International Journal of Practical Theology* 14 (2008): 47–67; Louw, "Creative Hope"; Louw, "HIV Pandemic"; William Lynch, *Images of Hope* (Notre Dame, IN: University of Notre Dame Press, 1974); Marcel, *Homo Viator*; Pembroke, "Witnessing to Hope"; Pruyser, "Maintaining Hope"; Root, "Theology of the Cross"; Stone and Lester, "Hope and Possibility"; Whelan, "Human Ground of Hope."

89. See Pembroke, *Pastoral Care in Worship*, 96; Pembroke, "Witnessing to Hope," 436.

90. Root, *Promise of Despair*, 142.

goes on to say, "Despair and hope are inseparable. One can never understand what hope is really about unless one wrestles with despair. . . . [Hope] means wrestling with despair . . . but never allowing it to have the last word."[92] Central to Kwan's argument is Moltmann's dialectic of the cross and resurrection: "Hope takes shape amidst difficulties, and losing a sense of control over the future is often the beginning of hope."[93]

Pruyser, drawing on Gabriel Marcel, emphasizes that hoping presupposes a tragic situation, a situation of being trapped. To hope, one must have a tragic sense of life, an undistorted sense of reality, a degree of modesty with respect to the cosmos/nature, a feeling of commonality with others, and some capacity to resist impulsive, unrealistic wishing (more akin to optimism).[94] Hope, then, is the movement from the experience of imprisonment, constriction, and isolation to openness and communion. Several researchers and thinkers emphasize that hope is deeply related to suffering, death, and illness.[95] For example, Louw writes, "Hope is only hope within suffering, not a flight from suffering, nor attempting to bypass suffering."[96] And William Stringfellow has said, "Hope is known only in the midst of coping with death. Any so-called hope is delusionary and false without or apart from the confrontation with the power of death . . . . [R]esistance to death is the only way to live humanly in the midst of the fall."[97]

In his thoughtful analysis of hope in the face of death, Herbert emphasizes the proximity of hope and hopelessness: "Because both are born out of the same climate of uncertainty, the relationship between them is more ambiguous than simply one of opposites."[98] Drawing on the work of theologian William Lynch, Herbert suggests that there is a creative kind of hopelessness that forms an important part of the hoping process. He argues that hope can properly

91. Kwan, "Interrogating 'Hope,'" 65.

92. Ibid., 65. Kwan quotes Cornell West, *The Cornell West Reader* (New York: Civitas, 1999), 554. He also draws on Moltmann for his discussion of the intersectionality of hope and hopelessness.

93. Kwan, "Interrogating 'Hope,'" 65–66.

94. Pruyser, "Maintaining Hope," 122.

95. Richardson, "Where There Is Hope, There Is Life," 79; Louw, "Pastoral Care and the Therapeutic Dimension of Christian Hope." See also La Mothe, "What Hope Is There?," 493: "Hope contains confidence and doubt; this confidence energizes people to achieve their dream but not despair if they fail."

96. Louw, "HIV Pandemic," 110–11.

97. William Stringfellow, quoted in Sheryl A. Kujawa-Holbrook, "Love and Power: Antiracist Pastoral Care," in *Injustice and the Care of Souls: Taking Oppression Seriously in Pastoral Care*, ed. Sheryl A. Kujawa-Holbrook and Karen B. Montagno (Minneapolis: Fortress Press, 2009), 16.

98. Herbert, *Living Hope*, 26.

come into being in a way that is free of the absolutizing instinct only when the reality of limitation is acknowledged: "Good hope is not deluded by fantasy, and the one who hopes accepts that certain projects are helpless and not worth hoping for. In this way hopelessness 'becomes a ground'; . . . however, . . . problems [can] occur when hopelessness invades our hope in a way that is simply destructive."[99]

Serene Jones engages the relationship of hope and its negations spatially by imaging how death lives within God. In the face of despair, death, and suffering, hope is enabled by opening to the larger space within which negating dimensions of being exist:[100] "What happens in the Godhead when Christ, part of the Godhead, dies? . . . On the cross, God takes this death into the depths of God's self. . . . Thus the trinity holds death . . . . When Christ is crucified, God's own child dies. For the God who sent this child into the world bearing the hope of God's eternal love, this death is the death of hope, the hope that the people who see the child will believe."[101]

The paradox of cross and resurrection stands at the heart of the relationship between despair and hope in the thought of theologians of the cross. Recalling Luther's Heidelberg Catechism, Andrew Root argues that despair is basically a prerequisite of true hope. Humans must utterly despair of their own ability before being enabled to receive God's grace and hope. "Luther paradoxically finds some hope in despair and some meaning in nihilism. . . . God is present right in the middle of the nihilism of despair."[102] Hope comes through death, through despair: "All those who despair can, in the power of the Spirit, take hope for they are enveloped in the love of the Father and the Son. Through their despair God is coming to them."[103] Similarly, Jean Stairs posits that it is when we as humans face our own helplessness and limitations, when we come up to that against which we have no control, when we are "in the heart of death, narcissistic egoism dies so that the soul can be awakened and set free for authentic love of self, others, and God."[104] It is fundamentally in the face of the

99. Ibid., 26.

100. Serene Jones, *Trauma and Grace: Theology in a Ruptured World* (Louisville: Westminster John Knox, 2009), 148. John Swinton also suggests a more spatial or embodied construction of hope in his emphasis upon evil and suffering being absorbed and transformed within Christ and within communities of faith who live out such a call—to absorb and transform negations within communities of friendship and solidarity. Swinton, *Raging with Compassion*, 67.

101. Jones, *Trauma and Grace*, 148–49.

102. Root, "A Theology of the Cross and Ministry in our Time," 191.

103. Root, *Promise of Despair*, 144.

104. Jean Stairs, *Listening for the Soul: Pastoral Care and Spiritual Direction* (Minneapolis: Fortress Press, 2000), 92.

experience of God's absence "in voicing despair that the soul is most keenly alive in the reality of God. The power of hope is enacted in the utterance of despair."[105]

In the health care fields, Dufault and Martocchio and Herth all highlight the dialectical relationship of hope and hopelessness in their research on the experience of patients in health care settings.[106] As well, in her summary of the health care research on hope, Stoner shows that hope is commonly related to experiences of captivity and despair.[107]

HOPE BEYOND BINARIES OF DESPAIR AND OPTIMISM

While there is not much written specifically on the theme of hope beyond the binaries of despair and optimism, it emerges in the absence of discussions regarding hope's relation to optimism and despair and from the character of experiences included in the literature on hope.[108] Indeed, the need for thinkers and researchers to critique hope's relationship to optimism in part grows out of a reaction against certain philosophical movements of the nineteenth century that imagined a progressive, linear, and inevitable movement of history toward its fulfillment. When hope is related to optimism in history, some detect this naive and ultimately harmful philosophical perspective is operative beneath the surface. At the same time, the data suggest that despair, hopelessness, and negations in life can be important in experiences of hope. Is it necessary to make such strict distinctions between hope in relation to optimism or to despair? Why

105. Ibid., 96–97. Wright and Strawn in dialogue with psychoanalyst Peter Shabad raise a similar point, arguing that mourning and lament are necessary for hope to be reborn. While the ground of hope may be a transcendent vision of God, the importance of mourning and lament cannot be overstated. We need to release our true selves before God. Ronald W. Wright and Brad T. Strawn, "Grief, Hope and Prophetic Imagination: Psychoanalysis and Christian Traditions in Dialogue," *Journal of Psychology and Christianity* 29, no. 2 (2010): 152–54. In his study on the spirituality of the Psalms, Walter Brueggemann argues that the psalms are "finally an act of hope. But the hope is rooted precisely in the midst of loss and darkness, where God is surprisingly present. The Jewish reality of exile, the Christian confession of crucifixion and cross, the honest recognition that there is an untamed darkness in our life that must be embraced—all of that is fundamental to the gift of new life. The Psalms are profoundly subversive of the dominant culture, which wants to deny and cover over the darkness we are called to enter." Walter Brueggemann, *Spirituality of the Psalms* (Minneapolis: Fortress Press, 2002), xii.

106. Kaye Herth, "Abbreviated Instrument to Measure Hope: Development and Psychometric Evaluation," *Journal of Advanced Nursing* 17, no.10 (1992): 1251–59; Dufault and Martocchio, "Hope and Its Spheres and Dimensions."

107. Stoner, "Measuring Hope," 225.

108. Duane Bidwell, "Eschatology and Childhood Hope: Reflections from Work in Progress," *Journal of Pastoral Theology* 20, no. 2 (2010): 109–127; Bourgeault, *Mystical Hope*; Serene Jones, "Hope Deferred," in *Trauma and Grace*, 127–50.

the need for such binary categories in order to locate hope or to place it over and against something deemed other or even contaminating? Is it not possible that hope emerges within, beyond, inclusive of optimism or despair? Some of the literature points to this possibility and suggests an openness to multiple ways that hope may or may not relate to both optimism and despair and may do so simultaneously or not at all.

HOPE AND TEMPORALITY

As Jean Stairs posits, "How we understand time is a profoundly theological matter."[109]

One of the most common ways to construe hope is to consider it to be about time and more specifically about the future. Some believe hope refers to the individual's or the community's relationship to its own future, which can, in turn, affect the interpretation of the individual's or community's present and past. Some believe it to be more about the relationship of eternity to time or God's relationship to time. They emphasize an eschatological understanding of history, which practically affects the human experience of time by placing it within a larger context. Still others question the assumption that hope is in the first place about a relationship to temporality at all and choose instead spatial metaphors and relational understandings that suggest an opening of multiple horizons in the experience of hope.

HOPE AS THE HUMAN RELATIONSHIP TO TIME, ESPECIALLY FUTURITY

Several sources identify the importance of perceptions of the future in the experience of hope.[110] Most of these consider that hope is related to, but not exclusively determined by, feelings about the future. In her extensive study of research on hope within health care, Marcia Stoner identifies "future orientation" as one of four of the most common themes discussed in the research on hope.[111] The human relationship to time, specifically as this enables openness to the future, is central to these perspectives on hope and temporality.

Both Capps and Carson describe hope as engaging in action to facilitate meeting future expectations.[112] Stone also suggests that openness to one's own

109. Stairs, *Listening for the Soul*, 120.

110. A. T. Beck, M. S. Brown, R. J. Berchick, B. L. Stewart, and R. A. Steer, "Relationship between Hopelessness and Ultimate Suicide," *Focus* 4, no. 2 (2006): 291–96; Capps, *Agents of Hope*; Jay Gary, "Creating the Future of Faith: Foresighted Pastors and Organic Theologians," *Dialog* 43, no. 1 (2004): 37–41; Herth, "Abbreviated Instrument to Measure Hope"; Nowotny, "Assessment of Hope"; Stone and Lester, "Hope and Possibility"; Stoner, "Measuring Hope."

111. Stoner, "Measuring Hope," 225.

future is enabled by trusting anticipation for that future. "Hope represents a future filled with possibilities, and it offers a blessing. Used theologically, the word hope is a recognition of possibilities that lie ahead, a trusting anticipation of a time when troubles lessen or end, an investment in tomorrow that holds promise."[113] In working with clients, therefore, it is important to engender hope by projecting the possibilities of the *not-yet* in the future.[114]

For those working with clients recovering from trauma and in narrative therapy, there is the need for the client to speak and tell the story of the past in an effort to claim possibility in the present and future. The move to narrate past stories helps to open the present to the future in such a way that hope can emerge. While this therapy focuses on the past, it does so as a way to reframe the past story and to shift the plot so that it is not closed off and stuck in traumatic reenactment but rather becomes open to new possibility. Reframing past narratives allows hope to emerge in relation to the future.[115] A person's relationship to time and the ways of narrating time that feed hope are central to good therapeutic practice. In a similar way, Andrew Delbanco understands the meaning and impact of cultural narrative in opening up hope's relation to time: "If hope is indebted to the future, it is also invested with the past. Both temporal dimensions—past and future—continually impinge on the present. The past funds our ability to narrate the present as open to a hopeful future. The future locus is the ability to narrate our present as enabled by a hopeful past."[116]

HOPE AS THE RELATIONSHIP OF TIME TO ETERNITY, INCLUDING FUTURITY

This understanding of hope includes a focus on time and the human relationship with time. However, an eternal or eschatological horizon is what ultimately opens up the human's relationship with time.[117] In some cases, the

112. Carson, "Hope and Its Relationship to Spiritual Well-Being," 5; Donald Capps "Letting Loose of Hope: Where Psychology of Religion and Pastoral Care Converge," *Journal of Pastoral Care* 51, no. 2 (1997): 147.

113. Stone and Lester, "Hope and Possibility," 262.

114. Pruyser similarly says that people who hope are "future oriented in a special sense, namely by seeing reality as a process of unfolding and therefore essentially open-ended." Pruyser, "Maintaining Hope," 124.

115. See Lester, *Hope in Pastoral Care and Counseling*. See also Judith Herman, *Trauma and Recovery: The Aftermath of Violence—from Domestic Abuse to Political Terror*, 2nd ed. (New York: Basic, 1997).

116. Andrew Delbanco, *The Real American Dream: A Meditation on Hope* (Cambridge, MA: Harvard University Press, 1999), 69.

117. Walter Brueggemann, *Hope within History* (Atlanta: Westminster John Knox, 1987); Carrigan, "Where Has Hope Gone?"; Gary, "Creating the Future of Faith"; Grenz, "Hopeful Pessimist"; Herbert,

experience of hope in history is considered to be a foretaste of the fullness of time to come in the Parousia—a glimpse of eternity in time.[118] This is a perspective that envisages God's future impinging upon the present. Further, this perspective, in its Christian forms, is usually deeply linked with the story of Jesus' death and resurrection that shapes the narrative of hope's possibility in the future, both historical and eschatological. This perspective also often uses language of the *already* and the *not-yet* to point to God's fullness having already been revealed in Christ's resurrection as a foretaste of the not-yet of the final consummation of all things.

Several sources in this grouping reflect an eschatological perspective. Carrigan says, "Hope is nurtured and sustained by a hoping community, a community that anticipates the coming of God's kingdom. Within the community of faith, glimpses of fulfillment and moments of communion give shape to the present as well as the future."[119] LaMothe, drawing on Moltmann, argues that with Christian hope, people partially experience the future kingdom of God in the present when they act with love, compassion, and justice.[120] Grenz notes that Christian hope is particular and lays hold of an anticipated future promised in the Scriptures. Also, it is an eschatological hope, not merely temporal: "In hope the Christian lays hold of an eschatological horizon, for Christian hope is nurtured by eschatological vision,"[121] and "Eschatology, derived from the resurrection, reveals the hope principle embedded in the cross. Hope is actually resurrection hope."[122] The essence of hoping is an eschatological attitude.[123] Underwood draws on an eschatological understanding of hope: "The promise of resurrection is the kind of promise that

Living Hope; LaMothe, "What Hope Is There?"; Louw, "Pastoral Care and the Therapeutic Dimension of Christian Hope"; Louw, "HIV Pandemic"; Manoussakis, "Anarchic Principle"; Meyer, "Integrating Cognitive Theory"; Pembroke, "Witnessing to Hope"; Stone and Lester, "Hope and Possibility"; Ralph Underwood, "Hope in the Face of Chronic Pain and Mortality," *Pastoral Psychology* 58 (2009): 655–65; Weaver, "Senile Dementia"; Wright and Strawn, "Grief, Hope and Prophetic Imagination."

118. Louw, "Pastoral Care and the Therapeutic Dimension of Christian Hope," 88: "Hope has an eschatological dimension that anticipates Christ's parousia."

119. Carrigan, "Where Has Hope Gone?," 41.

120. LaMothe, "What Hope Is There?," 493.

121. Grenz, "Hopeful Pessimist," 309.

122. Louw, "HIV Pandemic," 108; Daniel Louw, "*Fides Quaerens Spem*: A Pastoral and Theological Response to Suffering and Evil," *Interpretation* 57, no. 4 (2003): 395: "Christian hope describes a new state of being: salvation and resurrection . . . . Within the tension between resistance and surrender, hope becomes visible and embodied via concrete acts of protest and co-suffering."

123. Weaver, "Senile Dementia"; Hall, "A Working Theology of Prison Ministry," 172: "Christian hope is based on Christ's resurrection but it is God's love as shown in the crucifixion that affirms . . . hope."

preceded itself, a future that invades the present, a time of distress, brokenness and ongoing pain."[124] Resurrection anticipates dynamic restoration in the future. Hope includes the idea of hoping for healing in life but also hope for new life, a resurrection hope.[125]

In other cases, faith in the God of the future opens up human possibilities in the future. This latter perspective is not so theologically prescriptive. Several writers emphasize the need to trust God into the future without needing to know details of how that future might look. Meyer draws on Lester, arguing that "transfinite hope is future focused and grounded in the trustworthiness and love of God."[126] Clarke advocates that the experience of suffering can propel people "back into life, into God's future." He writes that pastoral care for suffering people is to transform their energies of anger and pain "into a future-directed empowerment."[127] Neraas similarly argues, "At its best . . . hope holds stubbornly to a better future, without a precise time table or illusions about specific outcomes."[128] And Howard Stone expresses it this way: "Hope is regarded as the 'trustworthy anticipation of the future based on an understanding of a God who is trustworthy and calls us into an open-ended future.'"[129]

In the literature reviewed, only a couple of sources specifically emphasize heaven or an afterlife as the focus for hope. For the most part, the writers represented in this category are open to ideas about an afterlife but their thought is not focused especially on such ideas. Instead, the focus is trusting God with our future, which may or may not presuppose an afterlife.[130]

124. Underwood, "Enlarging Hope," 10.

125. Underwood, "Hope in the Face of Chronic Pain," 656–57. John Swinton also draws on the importance for eschatological hope to undergird the experience of hope in history: "Early Christians saw life in the present as transient and not definitive of human fulfillment, hope and expectation. . . . The hope of ultimate redemption and liberation from evil and suffering was always on the horizon; it was this future hope that enabled people to tolerate and make sense of suffering in the present." Swinton, *Raging with Compassion*, 37. "The church's practices bring into the present, if only partially, the possibilities of the eschaton." Ibid., 55.

126. Meyer, "Integrating Cognitive Theory," 20–21. Here, Meyer, like Herbert and drawing on Lester, emphasizes the trustworthiness of God for the future. Rather than anxiety shaping our anticipation of the future, trust in God can shape our anticipation of the future.

127. Michael J. Clark, "AIDS, Death and God: Gay Liberational Theology and the Problem of Suffering," *Journal of Pastoral Counseling* 21 (1986): 52.

128. Neraas, *Apprenticed to Hope*, x.

129. Howard W. Stone, "Summoning Hope in Those Who Are Depressed," *Pastoral Psychology* 46, no. 6 (1998): 432.

130. Brueggemann identifies the temptation to divide hope and history in such a way that the desire for an afterlife is considered to be the sum total of Christian hope: "The temptation among us is to split

HOPE IS NOT RELATED TO TEMPORALITY

One of the problems in the understanding that hope is always related to time, especially futurity, is that by default it excludes experiences of hope from people unable to think about their relationship with time. This is true of children, as Duane Bidwell suggests, and it is also true of those diagnosed with forms of dementia and other conditions. Can we really say that people who are children or have dementia or other conditions are unable to hope? Bidwell and some other researchers recognize that hope does exist in ways that do not require consciousness of temporality.[131] Bidwell argues that for children, hope is experienced as much (if not more) in the present tense, rather than in the future tense often emphasized in pastoral theology.[132] He summarizes their research on children's experiences of hope amid chronic illness in the following way: "Children's accounts of hopefulness . . . challenge the Christological, future-oriented, and individualistic eschatologies that have been primary in Christian traditions. The literature of pastoral theology, in particular, has not developed communal and present-oriented understandings of hope that are appropriate to caring with children. Making an intentional shift from longitudinal/temporal to latitudinal/spatial eschatologies could create opportunities to construct hope-generating practices that are more appropriate to spiritual care with children and more accountable to non-dual understandings of ultimate hope that manifests through the mundane."[133] While more research needs to be done, we believe that the same can be said of many others for whom a sense of temporality is focused primarily on the present. The Herth Hope Index demonstrates growing interest in exploring nontemporal notions of hope. While it does consider questions of temporality and futurity in the experience of hoping, it is concerned with expanding our understanding of hope in a way that is not focused on the human relationship with time.[134]

hope and history. As a result, we hold to a religious hope that is detached from the realities of the historical process. Or we participate in a history which ends in despair because the process itself delivers no lasting victories for the participants. It is precisely the wonder and burden of the biblical text that hope is relentlessly historical and history is cunningly hope filled." Brueggemann, *Hope within History*, 3.

131. Bidwell, "Eschatology and Childhood Hope"; Bidwell and Batinsky, "Abundance in Finitude: An Exploratory Study of Children's Accounts of Hope in Chronic Illness." *Journal of Pastoral Theology* 19, no. 1 (Summer 2009): 38–59.; Bingaman, "The New Anxiety"; Bourgeault, *Mystical Hope*; Carrigan, "Where Has Hope Gone?"

132. Bidwell, "Eschatology and Childhood Hope," 111.

133. Ibid., 122.

134. "The Herth Hope Index (HHI) is a 12-item, multi-dimensional index designed to measure global, non-time oriented sense of hope." K. A. Herth, "Herth Hope Index," IN-CAMS Outcome Database, 1989, http://www.outcomesdatabase.org/node/612.

A similar observation may be made of Stoner's hope scale. The focus of this hope scale is relational rather than temporal; that is, the relationships of self to self (intrapersonal), self to other (interpersonal), and self to all of life (global) have priority as the domains of hope. Reading temporality into hope, therefore, becomes a second step, rather than a defining aspect of hope. While a consequence of hope may be the opening up of the future, a sense of the opening of the future is not the sum total of hope. Within these intrapersonal, interpersonal, and global relationships, temporality may have a place.[135] However, temporality—a sense of past, present, and future—is not necessarily constitutive of hope.

Cynthia Bourgeault critiques time-bound understandings of hope. She elucidates mystical hope, which is the truest kind of hope, in terms of three characteristics: "1. [It is] not tied to a good outcome, to a future. It lives a life of its own seemingly without reference to external circumstance and conditions. 2. It has something to do with presence—not a future good outcome—but the immediate experience of being met, held in communion, by something intimately at hand. 3. It bears fruit within us at the psychological level in the sensations of strength, joy and satisfaction: 'an unbearable lightness of being.'"[136] Again, while openness to and anticipation of the future may be a consequence of hope, Bourgeault considers time's relationship to be secondary or consequential, rather than elemental of the experience of hope itself.

The emphasis here is on the opening up of the present to the eternal as more of a spatial category, instead of related to a fullness of the future. In Christian language, it would be possible to consider such experiences as *kairotic* moments, not primarily about glimpsing the future or experiencing the God of the future in the present. Rather, such moments open up the present to the eternal transcendence and fullness that is already among us and within which we already participate. Jesus saying, "The reign of God is among you," points to this possibility that imagines the fullness of God here and now meeting us, without the need to refer to some future culmination of time.

HOPE IN RELATIONSHIP

Does hope primarily exist as a phenomenon in relationship with one's self, in relationship with others/creation, or in relationship with the transcendent? As we have noted, the Stoner Hope Scale includes three domains of hope—intrapersonal, interpersonal, and global. These distinctions correspond to

---

135. Stoner, "Measuring Hope," 220.

136. Bourgeault, *Mystical Hope*, 9–10.

the distinctions emerging in this theme.[137] While there can be much overlap between these three domains when it comes to hope, the literature warrants each being discussed separately.

RELATIONSHIP WITH SELF

Stoner describes the relationship with self as the domain of hope grounded in interior resources and beliefs. It arises from within and is not dependent on transaction with another human being.[138] Others, who focus primarily on goal setting into the future as the basis of hope, often privilege the individual (self to self) and the individual's capacity to change her/himself or circumstance into the future.[139] Projecting a desired image of self into the future gives energy, direction, and vision to hope. While relationships with others or with the divine may affect the changing inner relationship of self to self, it is the relationship with the self that is primary. Capps, Snyder, and Clinebell (among others) reflect this perspective. The self of the present is firstly related to the self of the future. The dynamism of this relationship is what propels hope forward.

RELATIONSHIP WITH OTHERS/CREATION

Across the disciplines, we see a movement away from individually focused understandings of hope to more communally and relationally dependent models. Many focus on connectedness as a central aspect of hope.[140] This takes the form of friendship,[141] solidarity,[142] and bearing witness as central relational aspects of hope. Within the recovery model and other models of care, the relationship with caregivers is central for engendering hope. Caregivers are

---

137. Stoner, "Measuring Hope," 220.

138. Ibid.

139. Capps, *Agents of Hope*; Clinebell, *Counseling for Spiritually Empowered Wholeness*; Herth, "Abbreviated Instrument to Measure Hope"; Nowotny, "Assessment of Hope"; Snyder, *Handbook of Hope*.

140. Carrigan, "Where Has Hope Gone?"; Andrew Delbanco, *The Real American Dream* (Cambridge, MA: Harvard University Press, 1999); Ellison II, "'Late Stylin'"; Herbert, *Living Hope*; Herth, "Abbreviated Instrument to Measure Hope"; Louw, "Pastoral Care and the Therapeutic Dimension of Chritian Hope"; Neraas, *Apprenticed to Hope*; Nowotny, "Assessment of Hope"; Pembroke, "Witnessing to Hope"; Swinton, *Raging with Compassion*; Underwood, "Enlarging Hope"; Weaver, "Senile Dementia."

141. "In the midst of the silences, friends hope on our behalf, even when we cannot hope." Swinton, *Raging with Compassion*, 102. "Even when faith in God is lost friendship acts as intimation of divine possibility." Delbanco, *The Real American Dream*, 150, referring to Elie Weisel, *Town beyond the Wall*.

142. Sharon G. Thornton, *Broken yet Beloved: A Pastoral Theology of the Cross* (St. Louis: Chalice, 2002), 125–48.

often required to carry hope on behalf of those for whom they care.[143] Hope exists as an interpersonal possibility reflecting the extent to which humans as creatures are made for relationship, for love. When we are living in relationships of love, hope is present.[144] Isolation, lack of belonging, and lack of connectedness reflect that which distances from hope. The experience of connection with another, even in the midst of pain, opens up hope's possibility.

For an increasing number of thinkers and researchers today, the focus on belonging and community is the primary aspect of hope. Hope is created in community.[145] The importance of shared narratives and the retrieval of shared narratives is an essential part of the formation of community. For people of Jewish and Christian faiths, the Scriptures and the respective traditions are central to the creation of shared communal narratives. Neil Pembroke explores how Christians can reimagine hope in shared narratives as followers of Jesus, in shared actions of worship, in the Eucharist and prayer, in shared vision and sense of purpose.[146] Communion with others and with God creates hope.[147] The Hebrew Scriptures hold up the importance of shared narratives as the ground for hope. It is by narratives that we remember who and whose we are. It is by narratives that we are reminded of things that are eternally true. It is by narratives that we *remember* the future through narrating the work of God's saving work in the past. Without communal remembering, enacting, and narrating, there would be no hope, no shared vision or understanding, no way to see beyond the horizon of the immediate.

In summarizing the findings of his research on hope in childhood, Bidwell also emphasizes the constitutive role of relationships and community for hope: "This work has led me to understand hope as a social artifact that emerges 'between' people and communities prior to becoming appropriated and

143. See Nora Jacobson and Dianne Greenley, "What Is Recovery? A Conceptual Model and Explication," *Psychiatric Services* 52, no. 4 (2001): http://ps.psychiatryonline.org/article.aspx?articleid=85752. See also the work of Patricia Deegan at her website, https://www.patdeegan.com. See also Neraas, *Apprenticed to Hope*,38: "The therapist proposed that my friend borrow hope from her for a while, until the day came when she could take it into herself enough to be warmed by its flame."

144. Swinton, *Raging with Compassion*, 198; Richardson, "Where There Is Hope," 79.

145. Neraas, *Apprenticed to Hope*, 43: "Hope arises in community and can be shared and passed along in a current of love." Delbanco, *The Real American Dream*, 236.

146. Neil Pembroke well illustrates this perspective in his book *Pastoral Care in Worship*. See also Grenz, "Hopeful Pessimist," 305. Grenz focuses on the constitutive community in which narratives are shared. See also Carrigan, "Where Has Hope Gone?," 41: "Hope is nurtured and sustained by a hoping community, a community that anticipates the coming of God's kingdom."

147. Swinton, *Raging with Compassion*, 125.

internalized by individuals as a resources they can access at will. Thus, I conceptualize hope as a contextual spiritual resource that manifests through the interplay of social processes, and individual's internal and external resources, and an active transcendent presence."[148]

A related area we wish to highlight here is only touched upon briefly in the literature but is becoming increasingly important. It is the focus on a relationship with creation. Increasingly, the human relationship with nonhuman creation is articulated as that which engenders and ignites hope. Some of the theory on hope emphasizes the relationship with nature as an indicator of hope.[149] To discover oneself in moments of awe at the sight of creation's beauty engenders hope. To know oneself as connected with other creatures in symbiotic, interdependent relationships can feed hope's possibility.

RELATIONSHIP WITH TRANSCENDENCE

To some extent, the relationship of hope with the transcendent is implicit in some of the other themes that have been discussed. Writers in this grouping consider that the relationship with the divine, the transcendent Other, opens up hope.[150] Though somewhat prescriptive in his description, Swinton argues that ultimately "the only source of real hope" is "faith in a loving God who will bring liberation and redemption."[151] So, too, with LaMothe, what enables radical hope is a relationship of trust in God.[152] To experience the transcendent God—whether through worship, creation, other people, and so on—is an experience of hope. Maynard argues that it is when we experience transcendent love that hope is enabled and loss is transfigured.[153] Similarly, Pruyser describes hope as the presence of God in life and in death.[154] There is the sense that the experience of hope, whenever and however it happens, is the experience of being met by transcendence. Hope is the evidence of Divine presence.

148. Bidwell, "Eschatology and Childhood Hope," 110–11.

149. Jacobsen and Greenley, "What Is Recovery?"

150. See Grenz, "Hopeful Pessimist"; Herbert, *Living Hope*; Nowotny, "Assessment of Hope"; Weaver, "Senile Dementia."

151. Swinton, *Raging with Compassion*, 15.

152. LaMothe, "Reflections on Pastoral Leadership," 10–21.

153. Maynard, *Transfiguring Loss*, 9–10.

154. Pruyser, "Maintaining Hope,"130.

DEFINING HOPE

While our discussion so far could be used to highlight the tensions and conflicts present within schools of thought around the topic of hope, it is more helpful to receive the findings of this literature review as a demonstration of the multivalent, mysterious, and dynamic experience of hope in life. From the findings, it would be easy to surmise that no single *prescriptive* definition of hope can suffice, for any single definition would tend to privilege one or the other axis present in discussions of hope. At the same time, we believe it is possible, even helpful, to propose a working *descriptive* definition of hope that can help open up space for multiple ways to recognize hope's presence in life. The definition is inclusive of all the aforementioned axes and tensions, privileging hope as a specific type of experience that is embedded in multiple layers of relationality. *Hope is the experience of the opening of horizons of meaning and participation in relationship to time, other human and nonhuman being, and/or the transcendent.*

In relation to the preceding discussion, we can say many things about this understanding of hope. The working definition proposed here describes the experience of hope without identifying any of the specific origins, objects, or agents of hope to which it may—or may not—be related. Questions of origin, object, and agency can be read into experiences of hope. In fact, such readings no doubt will affect the experience of hope itself. However, as a descriptive definition, it rejects prescriptive ways of determining origin, object, and agency in relation to hope. Our definition can include experiences related to optimism and to despair without being bound in relation to either binary. Similarly, our definition can include the human and/or divine relationship with time and history. It is not, however, limited to specific assumptions regarding relationship of hope with temporality. Our definition of hope can be interpreted spatially and as an experience that is available for those who are not conscious of either time or the future. The definition can include theistic and nontheistic understandings while also being available to understandings of the human relationship to the self, to other people, to creation, and to the Divine.

Throughout the foregoing discussion, there are many different assumptions functioning regarding the state of being presupposed in the human spirit in order for hope to emerge. For example, for some, the state of being required for hope to flourish is related to human activity, empowerment, willing, and doing that are manifested in a drive toward the future. Others highlight the biblical idea of hope as expectant waiting. In this case, one must be in a posture of receptivity and expectant waiting upon God to experience hope. Finally, others emphasize trust, consent, and *just being* as the postures of being that most relate to hope. In our descriptive definition of hope, all these postures of being can be the ground upon which hope emerges. In fact, our definition allows for the possibility for all these postures of being to intermingle and be part of hope.

Within our proposed definition of hope, the focus on "the opening of horizons of meaning and participation" needs to be unpacked further. First, the notion of "opening of horizons of meaning" points to a perceived enlarging of a context of interpretation within which one reads phenomena, including the experience of oneself in relation. The term suggests an opening up of space, a broadening of perspective. While the language does suggest Gadamer's focus on horizons of meaning, it is not specifically related to Gadamerian thought.[155] What is most appealing about the image of "opening horizons of meaning" is how it reflects a shift within which one is relocated in a broader context; a vista opens up that had not been previously perceived. This relocation, this shift, this change and opening of perception is held up as a central element in the experience of hope.

Second, our definition emphasizes "horizon of meaning and participation." While *meaning* was not a theme identified in our review, throughout the literature there is a common emphasis on meaning as a shifting perception. How we read the data of life and how we interpret ourselves in relation to the data and to a larger whole are elemental questions related to hope in its many manifestations. The emphasis on meaning in our definition is not intended to privilege a cognitive process, though it can include this. Rather, the emphasis on meaning as a horizon reflects the extent to which one's location shapes one's perception and interpretation of life. One's location affects the horizon of meaning available to perception. It is when one's perspective is shifted and opened up that hope is experienced. The emphasis on "participation" is related to meaning and could be included within its purview. However, we include "horizon of participation" specifically in the definition because it draws attention to the ways meaning is embodied in the multivalent relationships within which we participate. The emphasis on participation suggests that hope is related to discovering oneself to be participating in a larger whole, connected to, engaged by, and in relationship with that within which one is already embedded but sees with new eyes.

It may be most accurate to say that this descriptive definition offers a hermeneutic of hope, a lens by which to interpret the presence of hope as it

---

155. Gadamer, Hans-Georg *Truth and Method* (London: Sheed and Ward, 1975), 267–273.

exists in life and potentially a lens by which to discern a process by which to facilitate hope. In the latter case, this definition suggests that hope's emergence has to do with the opening up of connection, relationship, participation, belonging, contexts of meaning. This opening of horizons of meaning and participation—this hope—may come through a person's increased sense of agency and empowerment to achieve future goals. It may come through making a meaningful connection with another person where trust, understanding, and mutuality are present. It may emerge when one experiences a sense of belonging in a community where narratives and a sense of vision are shared. The opening of hope may come when stories of past trauma are *heard into speech*, cathartically opening up horizons of meaning for the future. It may come in relationship to the community of creation when a sense of awe makes one aware of participating within the interconnectivity of all things. It may emerge in experiences of being met by transcendence in prayer, in worship, in acts of justice and mercy, when eyes are opened and the world is seen with eyes of love. All of these examples of hope's emergence point to different ways horizons of meaning and participation are opened up in relation to time, to other humans and creatures, and to the transcendent.

As we move into exploring diverse narratives of hope over the next few chapters, we will explore different ways to recognize hope within contexts of adversity and struggle. As with the definition itself, these narratives are invitational and suggestive. In no way are these narratives of hope intended to be exhaustive. They reflect diverse manifestations of hope in situations of adversity where we would least expect hope to be present. The reader is encouraged to look more deeply into her or his own life and there to discover experiences of hope that might yet feed and nourish the soul.

3

Hope as Fight

Not that I have already obtained this or have already reached the goal; but I press on to make it my own because Christ Jesus has made me his own. Beloved, I do not consider that I have made it my own; but this one thing I do: forgetting what lies behind and straining forward to what lies ahead, I press on toward the goal for the prize of the heavenly call of God in Christ Jesus.
Phil. 3:12-14

Jess[1] was a fun-loving twenty-eight-year-old single mother of three on the night when she went out with friends to have some well-deserved fun. She remembers the details of that night twenty-two years ago as if it were yesterday—the games they played, the dancing, the laughing, the gossip and drama of relationships unfolding. On their way home, as they drove along the highway that cuts through their city, the accident happened. While she has shared this part of the story many times, she still cannot remember anything past the moment when she opened the window and put her hand out to surf the wind on that warm summer night. The next morning, the newspaper headline read something like "Three Injured, One Critically—Drunk Driving Suspected."

She remembers waking up a few days later in the trauma center. The impact of the accident had caused major damage to her spine, breaking it at the C5 and C6. She had tubes coming out everywhere and monitors beeping and buzzing all around her. Worst of all, while she had heard people tell her this, she slowly came to realize she could not feel her legs nor move her body. As the

---

1. This story is based on a story received through interviews and ongoing discussion. The person upon whose story this one is based ("Jess") has reviewed the chapter, provided input, and given permission for the use of her story. Details of the story, including names, locations, and time lines, have been changed in order to ensure confidentiality.

routine of being fed and turned, bathed and toileted continued, the reality of what she was facing started to settle in, first as panic and then as depression and anger. How could she do the all the things she had always done? How could she ever care for her kids, hold a job, make dinner, go shopping, or tuck her youngest into bed? How could she even leave the hospital?

One evening, after a visit with her kids and the cousin who was caring for them, she felt overwhelmed with hopelessness, unable to imagine how life could go on for her. It would be so much easier to end it, she remembers thinking. What future did she have? Just pain and torment and grief over the loss of everything she had ever known. "I was praying through this whole time, you know," Jess now tells me. "And I actually didn't blame God or anything, but I just kept calling out to God in desperation, "Help me! Help me!"

She describes how she would turn inward, shut down, and numb out but then feel surges of resentment:

> During this time, for a while, I kinda went between feeling like giving up and killing myself to feeling really mad about stuff and resentful of people. I would feel resentful when people came in and did everything so easily—stupid stuff like picking up a pencil or a Kleenex—and here I was only able to sip from a straw when someone else held a cup for me. Sometimes I got really mad that I ended up so badly injured and the driver, who was charged with drunk driving, walked away without an injury. Sometimes I got really caught in that, mad at him. [pause] Also, I thought a lot about all the what-ifs: What if one if my kids had been sick and I had to stay home that night? What if I had sat where I was going to sit in the car instead of where I did? What if I had not gotten into the car at all? . . . Yeah, [pause] and I could get really mad when I thought about what I had before the accident and what I didn't have after. It all made me fall deeper into a pit.

Jess goes on to describe that sometime between her thoughts of suicide, numbing out in depression, and raging against everything she began to realize that this was no way to live. She recognized that God did not want suicide for her. Sure, it was the easy way out, but then what? It would leave her kids in a worse situation, and it would mean that the bad stuff in life had won out. Eventually, she made a vow to God promising that she would not give in to this temptation. She would not kill herself. But that meant she needed to figure out how to live differently. She needed to figure out how to stop bouncing between despair and rage. Neither her anger nor her depression was very useful for her; instead, they were really making life miserable. She recalls one day realizing that she could choose not to be angry and not to be depressed:

> Crazy as it sounds, it was like it suddenly dawned on me that I could probably choose not to be mad or even depressed. Somehow I could choose against that. Sure, no one would blame me if I stayed stuck there. I had all the reasons in the world to stay mad and depressed, but that's no way to live. So somehow I began to think about things differently. . . . I think of this as God kinda prodding me along. I could keep on the road I was on to oblivion, or I could figure out some things that I could do and begin to work to make them happen. It was like I began to realize that these were demons I was fighting—despair and anger. They were real and were taking their toll on me, and I had to fight against them. God helped me with that. But that took its time with lots of failure in between.

As Jess shares her inner journey through this time, she describes how important it was for her to realize what she needed to *fight against*. She also shares an image of herself in the future that came to her at this time that revealed what to fight for into the future. The image was of Jess showering herself and got her through almost two years of therapy. For Jess, the worst part of the accident was ending up so dependent on others, especially being bathed and toileted by others. To shower herself, without assistance from others, was a simple but powerful and representative future act that drew her forward. Each day in physiotherapy and with all her daily exercises, she would focus on doing just one thing that would help her reach her goal.

Jess remembers that she sometimes felt as if nothing was progressing, and she would experience the demons starting to taunt her to give up. When asked about how she dealt with this, she recalls that her prayer life made all the difference. Every day, she would ask God to help her stay focused on her goal and to resist the temptations that sometimes erupted. Step-by-step Jess worked toward her goal until finally, many months later, she did it: in a special chair, with a custom-made shower head and stall, she showered herself. Recalling how she had worked her way to her goal of the shower stall gave her hope and motivation to try other things, like washing dishes and cooking, which with a lot of hard work, she also mastered.

When she talks about the challenges of this time, she is mindful also that the demons of despair and depression still can taunt her sometimes. She never presumes to be wholly out of the woods. But her experience has helped clarify for her what she needs to do when she feels tempted to give up and how her faith in God plays a central role in helping to keep her on the right track. She always had and continues to have a sense of God's presence with her.

One of the most important parts of Jess's inner healing and something that she says also influenced her ability to hope was a dream, or more aptly a visitation, that came to her a few years after the accident. In the dream, the man who had caused the accident came to her and asked her forgiveness for the pain and damage he had caused. It was all very real. She saw him, heard his plea for forgiveness, and straight to his face, she granted him forgiveness. She had not realized until that time how much she still had to let go, how much the burden of unfairness still weighed on her. A big shift happened for Jess through the forgiveness shared in the dream. She felt freer and lighter, even more able to hope. While the dream itself had a powerful effect, what confirmed for her the sacred profundity of this mysterious nighttime exchange was the communication she received the next day. Jess learned that the man who came asking for forgiveness had died on the night of her dream—in a car accident, of all things. For Jess, this experience of visitation and forgiveness marked another turning point in her journey of hope.

It is twenty-two years now since the accident. Jess's kids have grown up and are doing well. She sees them all regularly and has a growing number of grandchildren, who like to climb on her and her wheelchair and zoom around sometimes. They have the usual arguments and tensions and laughs. She has her friends to hang out with and the community where she lives. Both can get gossipy and full of drama sometimes, but she figures that is the way it is with people. There is grace in the normality of it all—and hope, too.

Reflecting with Jess

How is hope present in Jess's story? How does her story reflect manifestations of hope in life in the face of devastating loss? How does it relate to our definition and to practices of care? What are some of the cautions and possibilities that Jess's story holds?

When asked, Jess has incredible clarity regarding the ways hope was present for her through this difficult time in her life. In no way does she suggest it was easy, linear, or straightforward. Hope was a process that unfolded, often without the assistance of any one caregiver, though various friends and health professionals were part of the journey. The gradual emergence of hope involved all sorts of currents within herself, her faith journey, and her sense of herself in relation to life and to those around her.

In many ways, Jess's story of fighting for and against something—fighting to be able to shower herself and fighting against depression and giving up—includes the most common way hope is understood in the caregiving literature. In this case, hope exists in the dynamic relationship between her present experience of paralysis and her future goal of showering herself, mediated by empowered agency. Capps's, Snyder's, and others' similar definitions of hope and understandings of care are easily recognizable here.[2] Helping to facilitate hope in this case first means supporting and empowering Jess to recognize herself as an active agent able to make choices for a desired future and choices against all that could undermine its possibility—that is, being overwhelmed by hopelessness and giving up. It means supporting her to establish achievable goals and breaking down the means to reach these goals step-by-step. It means helping to establish practices that keep at bay the temptations to give up and turn away from a sense of desire for the future.

Central to Jess's experience of hope is the emergence of choice and her ability to choose for and against certain inner reactions that had been keeping her captive. When she discovers a way to choose for or against anger and depression, not only does she experience an empowering sense of agency, but also with that, possibilities for life open up in ways that had not been present before. Prior to this time, she had struggled with a sense of fatalism that seemed to bind her to exist in a hopeless dark pit without any sense of choice or possible change for the future. The emergence of choice, of empowered agency, enables her to distance herself from the many reactions and naturally occurring emotions stirring within her in response to her devastating experience. She need not be defined or confined by these. While being mindful that her responses are natural and she need not judge herself for such feelings, she also realizes that she can choose another way. She can begin to hope—and does so, with God as her helper.

Another important point that emerges from Jess's goal-oriented hope is the extent to which the goal itself is real, true, and "temporal" but also holds within it symbolic spiritual power related to her sense of self, the possibility in life, and her relationship with God. For Jess, showering herself symbolizes a way to reclaim herself, her sense of self-sufficiency, her way of participating in

---

2. See "Hope and Agency" in chapter 2.

the world, her sense of boundary and integrity as a person. As well, it carries spiritual significance that points to her relationship with God, with whom nothing is impossible, not even a paralyzed woman showering herself in time. As well, this image represents a sense of purpose and meaning in her life. It stretches beyond being a historical achievable goal to becoming a symbol with transcendent connotation.

Not only is it important for Jess to have an achievable future in front of her, something to fight *for*, but also, with even greater clarity, she describes the importance of being able to recognize the demons she has to fight *against*. For her, this latter fight is a spiritual fight. Her battle against the demons of rage, depression, and defeat becomes clear to her in prayerful relationship with God, a very personal God. Knowing what she is fighting against enables her to have greater clarity, energy, and direction to know what she must fight for.

We can see how Jess's fight against giving up relates to the understanding that despair and hope cannot coexist, for despair will eat away and destroy hope.[3] On one level, through Jess's story, we see how hope and despair exist as opposing poles. Her work is to keep herself focused in the direction of hope, turning against the temptations of despair. When she finds herself turning in the direction of despair, she loses hope and has to find her way back. Over and over again, as she turns her face toward hope, she turns her back on despair and the temptations drawing her to give up.

In terms of our working definition of hope, we can see how the image of Jess showering herself stands before her as a goal which motivates her and calls her forward. Through this image, the present moment is opened up to the larger horizon of an achievable future within which she participates. This larger horizon of the future gives a context of meaning for her present actions. For Jess, hope is sustained in the present insofar as her present daily actions and smaller goals connect with the future larger goal. This larger goal shapes and interprets her present smaller goals, giving them significance and meaning. For her, it means that the daily fight for some muscle control over her fingers, hands, and then her arms is intrinsically linked to her vision of the future in which she is showering herself, which also symbolizes a transcendent sense of meaning, purpose, and relationship. When the relationship between her present daily smaller goals and future long-term goal is broken—when she feels like she is not getting anywhere in therapy—despair can threaten to undermine everything, including her relationship with God.

3. See See "Hope, Optimism and Despair" in chapter 2.

Central to Jess's experience of hope is the empowering experience of resistance and the fight against temptations that seek to turn her away from possibilities for her future and her relationship with God. These two are intrinsically linked. The power to resist and fight *against* energizes the power to fight *for* and move forward. When asked, she definitely emphasizes that her God-inspired ability to resist the powers of darkness and temptation in her life was the most important movement that made hope possible.

Jess's experience of hope does not end there. She speaks in many different ways about how hope is present for her through her journey. She thinks of it in terms of her relationship with God and her mindfulness of Divine Presence with her. Turning regularly to God helps her remember she is never alone and that she is ultimately accountable to God. Here, we can discern the enlarging of horizons from a more narrow to a more expansive perspective. Her relationship with God is that which draws her back to see herself and life in a bigger picture or context than what is immediate and material. It gives her perspective to claim her inner agency anew by choosing for and against certain things. Her decision not to commit suicide has everything to do with her faith and the vow she makes to God. Her vow enables her to transcend the immediate moments of desperation. She clings to this vow to help get her through. Here it is not so much her relationship with time but rather her relationship with the God of time and all things that opens her up to experience herself from a different angle and to find herself participating deeply in a relationship that transcends and opens up her immediate situation.

Jess speaks of hope also in terms of the experience of confession and forgiveness that happened in her dream visitation. In this, through a sacred rite of reconciliation between two people, eternity blesses and expands time with hope. She describes a shift happening within her that makes her feel released and unburdened from a weight she had not even realized she was still carrying so heavily. She finds herself hoping anew as horizons open in the space between her and the one who wronged her. Through this interaction between two people, we also see how Jess faces the trauma of her past, which continues to weigh her down in the present. As Jess pronounces words of forgiveness to the one who wronged her—words that carry transcendent resonance—her past is released and can no longer carry the pain and fragmentation of the trauma. In a greater way than was possible before this moment, her future opens up without the burden of the past weighing her down as it had.

Possibilities and Limits

One of the key issues that Jess's story raises is the importance of hope as fight, in terms of both fighting for something and fighting against or resisting something. Before further exploration of these dynamics and some necessary distinctions in understanding hope as fight, I will share a bit about where previous work on hope has taken me in this regard.

In previous work, I have critiqued the notion of hope as fight dependent on goals and outcomes, active human agency, and the priority of the will. I have argued that such notions of hope, when detached from a primal trust in Divine transcendence, have left hope's biblical moorings behind. Instead, I have said, such understandings of hope reflect the underlying currents of the modern West, in which humans seek mastery and control over human and nonhuman life.[4] With others, I have argued that part of the problem with such concepts of hope, especially as these exist in the North American context, is that they focus too much on the priority of the human will to enact control over life through technology and other means, so that any true sense of God or transcendence is eclipsed. I have suggested that the idea that hope is fundamentally about human agency, fighting for a goal and connecting the present to the future through specific pathways to that goal, can ultimately lead to the undermining of hope and the domination of despair. This is true, I argue, precisely because in such constructions of hope, human will and agency have usurped all notions of transcendence and trust in God. Human will and agency cannot bear the burden of hope for the future, though they can, of course, participate in it.

Over against modern Western notions of hope, I have outlined how hope as waiting—trusting, active, receptive, and attentive waiting in the world—is a more biblically based notion of hope that must be more fully reclaimed if we, as church and society, are to truly find a way to hope again. Ultimately, hope is fed by that which transcends and enfolds human will, agency, and desire. When we lose sight of this, we lose sight of true hope. Thus, any notion of hope as fight disconnected from any larger relationship cannot suffice, for it will result in turning in on itself. Rather, hope as fight must relate to a larger vision of that which includes and transcends the human will and active agency. While my previous work focused on a wider, more cultural critique of how hope functions societally, I am concerned here with exploring how, in the face of illness, trauma, and death, understandings of hope as fight may be helpfully discerned without losing sight of the potential pitfalls that such notions of hope

---

4. Pamela R. McCarroll, *Waiting at the Foot of the Cross: Toward a Theology of Hope for Today* (Eugene, OR: Pickwick, 2014).

present in our contemporary context. Indeed, I continue to hold to much of what I have previously argued. However, my learning from "Jess" has caused me to step back and take a more nuanced stance in terms of the important ways human agency, will, and desired future goals can be central to the ways hope is manifested in life, particularly as these are related to a dialogical faith in God or acknowledged participation in a larger whole. Jess's testimony has helped me clarify the importance of choice, as this relates to agency, will, and desire, and to further delineate both the possibilities and the pitfalls of hope as fight.

For our purposes in reflecting on experiences of hope as fight in the face of endings and traumatic transitions, it is helpful to explore the metaphor of fight as it dominates the public landscape in relation to illness and death. One of the most common metaphors for representing the human relationship with illness is that of fight or battle. Many would argue that this is the basis of the so-called medical model, where the goal of medicine, medical technology, and the pharmaceutical industry is to rid the world of the enemy of illness, the enemy of death. We see this assumption at work in the discourse of foundations lobbying for research funding, of medical professionals, and of patients and their families. There is public consent to the idea of fighting against illness as an enemy. Such a battle is considered to be an obvious and good thing. While argument can be made that this is an extension of a Judeo-Christian ethos that has long described death as the enemy, today this idea is disconnected from any specific faith perspective, though very much a given of the dominant secular North American culture.

On the positive side, many find meaningful ways to join in the battle against the enemy of disease through regular participation in annual walks, runs, wheels, and campaigns for any number of causes. People discover a sense of hope through the shared commitment and camaraderie of such actions as taking up the fight against cancer, heart disease and stroke, diabetes, obesity, HIV/AIDS, and so forth. By participating in such actions, people can discover meaningful ways of dealing with grief over the death or diagnosis of loved ones or their own experience of living with illness. Participating in such actions can be a helpful way of embodying the reality that while one may be marked by an illness, one cannot be defined by it. People can also experience a sense of empowerment to be able to take a leap of faith, to do something that may not ultimately make a difference in their own lives but will make a difference in the lives of others in the future. We see the common use of the fight metaphor in obituaries, the thumbnail stories of people's lives, where battles with various illnesses are held up as signs of identity, courage, and strength.[5] As well, the image of the heroic warrior courageously fighting the battle with disease and death is common in eulogies and narratives of people following death. These can all be meaningful ways to claim hope in the midst of the trials of life and death. It is important to honor this and hold it up as a means of hope and inspiration.

However, while the enacting of hope as fight can be a meaningful and important means to express hope's presence in life, it can also result in undermining hope and, instead, generate greater suffering and despair in the face of illness and death. The fight against the enemy of illness and death through science and research is commonly understood as the only or ultimate goal of medicine. When individual human narratives get read through this lens, much suffering can ensue, for the only apparent way of dealing with adversity in life appears to be that of resistance and fight. Through this lens, if one does not or cannot fight against the disease or a condition—especially if it is something for which much research money is allocated, like cancer—one can be looked upon with suspicion and concern. It is not uncommon for such concern to be raised by health care personnel at hospital rounds if a patient refuses treatment or seems to stop fighting in the face of illness. It can seem that outside the discourse of fighting against the enemy illness, there is no other means to hope in such situations. Where is there room for hope in the face of failure, finitude, and frailty? Where is there room for hope in the face of death, which whether we like it or not, meets us all? When fight against the enemy illness or death becomes an end in itself, disconnected from anything larger, hope is undermined, and despair, fear, and nihilism are given the final word.

I will never forget a man whose process of dying represents for me now the tragic ends toward which the *fight against* can lead. He was in his midfifties, diagnosed with cancer in several of his internal organs. As part of the palliative care team, I was asked to visit him because he was "agitated." My goal was to see how I could be present to help settle him or, at least, let him know that I could be with him if he was open to that. The medical team had indicated that he was exceedingly restless even though he did not complain about physical pain and his pain medications seemed to be working well. The chart also mentioned that he had no religious connection, that no one had come to visit, and that there

---

5. Here are a few examples from our local newspaper over a couple of days: "After making tremendous progress in her determined battle with a series of strokes"; "After a lengthy battle with heart disease"; "After a long but brave battle with cancer." *Toronto Star*, "Deaths," May 30, 2013, GT6. "After a tenacious and courageous battle with cancer"; "after losing a battle with cancer"; "after a year-long battle with cancer"; "—— had fought hard against the cancer that claimed him." *Toronto Star*, "Deaths," June 1, 2013, GT5. "After many years of fighting through several health issues"; "—— ended his courageous battle with cancer." *Toronto Star*, "Deaths," June 3, 2013, GT6.

were no family members or friends considered next of kin or substitute decision makers. There was no one to be called when he died, which everyone knew he would.

When I reached his room, he was pacing back and forth beside his bed, clothed in hospital robes, his feet bare. He had a desperate and confused look in his eyes and seemed unable to hold his gaze in one place. When I tried to speak with him, he seemed not to hear me and continued to pace, his hands restlessly reaching by his side. All the diagnostics indicated that this man would die at any moment. However, he kept pacing rigidly back and forth, confusing all those who could read his diagnostic reports. Sometimes he would sit on his chair momentarily, but as soon as he seemed to begin to sleep or lose consciousness, he would lurch forward, get up, and start to pace again, seemingly desperate to keep himself up, to keep himself alive.

I went in to see him a couple more times that week and found him in a similar state—pacing, agitated, and breathing more shallowly. The nurses and health care team had by that time begun to avoid him as much as possible. The combination of his overt suffering, agitation, and desperation fostered in all of us a sense of helplessness in the face of the inevitable. It was as if all those around could feel the fear, desperation, and hopelessness—the black hole in room eight. On a Saturday, one week after I had first met him, I was so disturbed by his discomfort and overt suffering that I called the palliative care physician at her home and pleaded with her to give him something that might settle him, that might make him more comfortable—something that might make all of us more comfortable. He died on the Tuesday the week following, after having collapsed on the floor while pacing.

None of us knew what was actually going on for this man on the inside. We did know, however, what was going on in each of us in relation to him. We knew that he represented something very fearful, and tragic for all of us on the health care team. He represented some of our worst fears about death and the experience of dying. I have often wondered since if there was a broken relationship or incident in his life that remained unreconciled and that was demanding his attention as he was moved restlessly toward his death. What more might I have done? I will never know. Several on the team felt that he was fighting against death right to his final breath, fighting against this enemy he felt stalking him and to which he could not consent. But what was worse was that he seemed to have nothing other than the desperate fight against death to keep him alive—no vision beyond death to settle him and no relationship in the world to give him comfort or to honor the meaning of his life as it had been lived.

The image of this man, agitated and relentlessly pacing to his death, bit deeply into my soul. I needed to stay present with it and shed tears from that pit of despair and the sheer meaninglessness of it all. I also needed to spend time in prayerful meditation, mindful of the larger horizon of existence, imaging him being lifted into a gentle and hearty love that was enfolding and holding him in his misery and terror.

How do we discern what to fight against and what to fight for? How do we discern when to stop fighting, when to surrender and consent to what is? Where does hope live within these dynamic movements of the soul in the face of all the adversity in life and death? One way or the other, when the fight for or against something becomes an end unto itself, without a reference to a larger horizon or sense of purpose and meaning than attaining or resisting the thing itself, hope is undermined, and despair, fear, and nihilism prevail. Any fight for a goal or resistance against an enemy, whether in the context of health or in contexts such as justice and peacemaking movements, must be connected with larger horizons of meaning if hope is to be truly present and generative. Without a larger horizon within which to interpret, the fight for or against something cannot alone generate hope, for the objects of the fight are not in themselves generative of hope. Sometimes the goal *for which* we fight helps provide the larger horizon shaping that *against which* we fight. However, even when balanced this way together (as in the case of Jess), a larger context within which to read both movements enables greater resilience of hope because its ultimate horizon transcends human ends as the source. When the thing we are resisting shuts us down from seeing beyond its demise, larger horizons of meaning are eclipsed, and hope is no longer present in the fight. So, too, when the goal we seek shuts us down from seeing beyond the sheer dynamism of reaching that goal, larger horizons of meaning are closed off, and generative hope is no longer present in the fight.

In considering our topic from within Christianity, it is important to note that hope as fight, whether for or against, includes particular content related to divine revelation embodied in Jesus. Hope as fight battles for justice, liberation, and peace for all. It fights for compassion, mercy, and forgiveness. It fights for healing and wholeness, for fullness of life and love. It fights for a sense of awe, thanksgiving, and worship. At the same time, within Christianity, hope as fight resists all that undermines life-giving and liberative currents in the world and within the human soul. It fights against injustice, tyranny, oppression, and destructive ways of being in relation to the self, the other, and creation. It fights against the powers of death that seek to undermine creaturely life in all its abundance and diversity. It fights against all that turns humans away from knowing themselves as intimately interrelated with all creatures within a much larger whole, created, redeemed, and sustained by an unfathomable Love. For those within Christianity, the content of what it is that hope fights for and against is known most fully through the life, witness, and Spirit of Jesus.

Conclusion

In times when hope needs to be hard fought, when expectations of life are shut down by accident, illness, or other major losses, what does hope-enabling care look like? As we have seen, in contexts where hope is present primarily as fight, practices of care exist in embodying and supporting people to discern what is worthy to fight for—that which feeds life, love, connectedness, gratitude, meaning, and transcendent possibility. Equally important is discernment regarding what to fight against—that which feeds death, fear, isolation, disconnection, resentment, and meaninglessness. In both the fight *for* and the fight *against*, the central component of hope is the participation of human agency to recognize the choices that are available and to choose for and against specific ways of being, thinking, and engaging life. Besides embodying relationships of care that manifest connectedness and compassion, practices of care can include constructing multiple possibilities of response to both the adversity and the possibility of life lived within the limits imposed. Underlying such practices is the affirmation that no matter how terrible the circumstances of life, choices can be made that bless rather than curse—that serve life rather than death. Further, such relationships and actions open up horizons that enable people to recognize their participation in much larger webs of relatedness and meaning that ultimately point to transcendent possibility.

While hope as fight can be a powerful and inspiring manifestation of hope in the face of adversity, without larger relationships with that which transcends the immediacy of the fight for or the fight against, the fight can turn in on itself and undermine hope's possibility in life. How hope as fight points beyond itself to larger horizons of possibility shapes the extent to which both resistance and goal-driven actions truly generate and participate in hope. Reinhold Niebuhr wrote what is now the well-known Serenity Prayer. It meaningfully addresses the distinctions between fight and acceptance in life and raises this struggle before God, the horizon that opens hope's possibility. Given to soldiers in World War II to carry with them in the trenches and offered now to many who attend twelve-step programs, it can give hope in times of confusion when we do not know what to fight for, what to fight against, and what to accept.

God, give us grace to accept with serenity
the things that cannot be changed,
courage to change the things that should be changed,
and the wisdom to distinguish the one from the other.
– 1943[6]

---

6. Reinhold Niebuhr, *Justice and Mercy* (Louisville: Westminster John Knox, 1974), front matter.

4

Hope as Meaning

I call on heaven and earth as witnesses against you today that I have set before you life and death, blessings and curses. Choose life so that you and your descendants may live, loving the Lord your God; obeying [God], and holding fast to [God]; for that means life to you and length of days.
Deut. 30:19–20a

Nicholas was the six-year-old only child of Pat.[1] I met the two of them and Pat's mother, Hazel, in the emergency room (ER) when I was doing rounds one Saturday morning. Nicholas had been having some bad headaches which were getting worse, so they brought him in to the ER. By the next morning, he was admitted to the pediatric intensive care unit (ICU) for observation while awaiting results of tests. Through much of this visit, he was sleeping but would pipe up sometimes and add to his mother's and grandmother's stories about him. They laughed about Nicholas's love of trees and tree climbing and how he'd scare his mom when he got up too high. They talked about how much he was enjoying grade one and how he never wanted to miss a day. They told stories about his many sleep toys and how he gave two of his favorite toys to the boy down the street, who was sad. They shared how perfect his vision was; he would often tell his mom, from blocks away, the letters on street signs. The visit was peppered with the joy that Nicholas brought to their lives and communicated how he was the "best thing that ever happened to" Pat.

When the medical team was called together to meet with the family and share test results, I sat with Pat and Hazel. The ICU doctor opened the meeting. "We are very sorry to say that the thing causing Nicholas so much pain is a tumor in his brain." She then pulled out the slide showing the tumor and

---

1. The story of Nicholas, Pat, and Hazel is based on a true story drawn from case notes and reflections from when I was a hospital chaplain. The names and details of the story, including timing and location, have been altered so as to ensure confidentiality for all parties.

outlined its shape. She continued, "Unfortunately the tumor is too deep for any surgery to be successful. We are also concerned that it is a kind of tumor that is very fast-growing." Questions surged forth from Pat and her mother: "But what can be done? What can we do?" After a pause, the doctor responded, "We can help with managing his pain. We can make him comfortable. We can probably shrink the tumor a bit with radiation and then get him stabilized enough to go home with you. But we don't know how long that will be able to last. He will likely need to be hospitalized again." Absorbing the information as it was coming to them, Pat and Hazel asked for clarification: "But what then? What kinds of treatments can he have? What's his prognosis?" The pediatric oncologist then took the lead in the meeting and repeated some of what had already been said. "Before he is released, he can have some radiation to see if the tumor can be shrunk a bit, to relieve some pressure. We can give him some pain meds for going home. But you need to know that the long-term prognosis doesn't look good." Sitting upright in her seat and leaning toward him, Pat pleaded, "What are you saying?! How long does he have?" Pushing his glasses up on his nose and tilting his head in compassion, the oncologist replied, "With kids I've known with this kind of tumor, it is usually a matter of months, though sometimes we can be surprised, and it may be a bit longer." Silence. The devastation in the room was palpable. How could this be?

After a while, the social worker spoke up. "Right now, Nicholas is exactly where he needs to be. It is important for you to be with him. You can tell him that the doctors are going to be able to help with the pain. We will meet again later this week and talk things through more then." Nodding, the women got up and went back to be with Nicholas. I joined them at the bedside later that evening. Nicholas wanted me to hear the prayer he liked to pray at night that he had just learned by memory: "Now I lay me down to sleep. I pray the Lord my soul to keep. Keep me safely through the night, and wake me with the morning light. Amen." He perked up his head for some praise, and his glance was met by three sets of tear-stained eyes smiling back at him. "Goodnight, Nicholas."

Nicholas was released a week later. He had radiation treatments that seemed to shrink the tumor somewhat. His pain was managed with medications, and he was able to go back to school and enjoy some of the things he had always enjoyed. Within seven weeks, however, he was readmitted to the ICU. His tumor had grown more quickly than expected, despite the radiation. Soon after admission, he was sedated and needed help to breathe. He did not have a lot more time. Pat talked with me about the previous few weeks—how good they had been, for the most part. She cried a lot and said how she'd tried to stay strong for Nicholas, tried to make it the best she could for him. She told me how mad she had been at first with the diagnosis. She couldn't believe it. But then, as time went on and some things in Nicholas started to change, she realized she needed to make this time as good as possible for him. She did not want to have any regrets. And then she went on:

> I've been thinking about this a lot, and I want to see what can be done. Nicholas has always been an incredibly generous kid—unusually able to share and someone who enjoys making other people happy. I need to do something to honor who Nicholas is. I want to do something to help others. If we are going through so much pain here, I want to see if we can at least do something to help others in their pain. It's how Nicholas is. It's how I want to be. I want all of his organs to be given to others who need them. His organs should be fine, I think, and good for others. Then others won't have to suffer like we are suffering right now.

I got to work on the arrangements. At that hospital at that time, the most common practice in situations of so-called organ harvesting was that loved ones would say their good-byes while patients were still on life-supporting machines. However, Pat was clear. She needed to say her final good-bye once Nicholas had actually died, after his organs had been taken, when there were no more tubes in him and instruments around him.

Within a couple of days, the time had come. The tumor had grown, and Nicholas was failing fast. Tests were done, and he was declared legally "brain dead" while machines kept his body alive. The organ transport team was called, and the operating room was prepared. It was late at night on a weekend. We arranged that I would accompany Pat and Hazel and wait with them during the procedure, and then the nurses would contact me to let us know when things were finished.

As we waited, Pat and Hazel told me of having been up the whole night and day before, stroking Nicholas's hair, telling stories about him, reminding him that he would be going to a better place, where he would not be sick and where he would have so many friends to play with all the time. They talked to him about how much their love for him and his love for them would keep them connected forever and how for Nicholas it would not feel long at all, and they would be joining him. Pat wondered aloud at who he would be helping with his organs. Much of the time was spent in silence, sitting together.

Then the call came from the nurses. We walked down the long, empty hallway to the operating room, opened the doors, and went in. There Nicholas lay, gently and delicately cared for—white sheets tucked up below his shoulders, hair brushed back, clean, smooth, soft skin. Having given his eyes, kidneys, liver, heart valves, and pancreas, he lay there, looking more peaceful than could have been imagined. Stroking his arm, kissing his head, saying good-bye, we stood around Nicholas's body in silence for a while, struck by the thinness of the veil between heaven and earth. Prompted by Pat's desire to hear Scripture, we gathered around Nicholas's bed, with the two nurses joining us, and I read parts of Psalm 139, adapted:

> O Lord, you have searched us and known us.
> . . . .
>   Where can we go from your spirit?
> Or where can we flee from your presence?
> If we ascend to heaven, you are there;
> if we make our bed in Sheol, you are there.
> If we take the wings of the morning
> and settle at the farthest limits of the sea,
> even there your hand shall lead us,
> and your right hand shall hold us fast.
> . . . .
>   For it was you who formed our inward parts;
> you knit us together in our mothers' wombs.
> . . . .
>   We are fearfully and wonderfully made.
> . . . .
>   Your eyes beheld our unformed substance.
> In your book were written
> all the days that were formed for us,
> when none of them as yet existed.
> . . . .
>   When we come to the end, we are still with you.

After anointing his head with oil and making the sign of the cross, I spoke words of blessing: "In the name of God who created you, Christ who prepares a place for you, and the Spirit who accompanies you, go in peace, Nicholas. We entrust you to God's care." Then grasping each other's hands, we prayed together, "Our Father, who art in heaven, hallowed be thy name. Thy kingdom come; thy will be done on earth as it is in heaven. Give us this day our daily bread, and forgive us our trespasses as we forgive those who trespass against us. And lead us not into temptation, but deliver us from evil. For thine is the kingdom forever." A moment of silence. "Amen." Pat leaned down and kissed Nicholas's face and hands, saying, "Good-bye, my sweet prince," and we left his body in the care of the nurses. Walking up the long hall in silence, we were speechless before the sacred mystery of what had just happened.

When I spoke with Pat in a follow-up call a few months later, she shared with me that she had received correspondence regarding the recipients of Nicholas's organs. His eyes had given a little girl sight. One of his kidneys went to a ten-year-old who had been waiting for ages for a match; the other had been given to someone after a devastating car accident. She had stories of all of the ways Nicholas's body had given life to other people. She also shared that "Nicholas's Tree" had been planted at the school with a full ceremony surrounding its planting. Next year, they would mark the day of his death with another ceremony at the tree. They chose one that would grow to be a good climbing tree; Nicholas would like that. She had given his sleep toys—all but one, which she kept for herself—to the little boy up the street. The nighttime prayer he had so proudly learned she found in a needlepoint kit and planned to spend meditative time making it over the next few months. Pat said it would be "something I can hang in my bedroom to remind me each night to say Nicholas's prayer." She and her mom were soon to walk in the pediatric cancer fund-raising walk, hoping to raise some money so others wouldn't have to go through the hell they'd been through.

"And what about you?" I asked. "How are you doing, Pat?" With that, she broke down in tears over the phone. She spoke through her tears:

> Sometimes I'm a mess. In fact, most of the time, I feel like a mess on the inside, despite how well everyone thinks I'm doing on the outside. . . . I still get thoughts about him in the ground, the cold ground. . . . What if there is no heaven? I get scared that there is no afterlife, and sometimes that really gets me. Other times he feels close, and heaven feels so real, and I think of him playing with friends and not suffering, and I feel better. I imagine him in light and love and warm and safe, looking just like he did in his grade one photo, happy and full of life. I'm holding on by a string sometimes. . . . When I think about my life before Nicholas, I realize again and again how much he changed me—like he taught me to love like I could never have imagined was possible. . . . But that's what is so painful now: I just want to love him now. *[weeping]* . . . I do love him now.

. . . It's hard. . . . I want to hold onto how much I've been changed by being his mom. . . .

    [weeping] But it's hard.

We talked for a while, during which time I affirmed that her vision of Nicholas bathed in light and love was a vision of God's promise that she can trust. After I gave her my number and that of the parents' bereavement group, we said our good-byes. "God be with you, Pat."

REFLECTING WITH PAT

How is hope present in the story of Nicholas, Pat, and Hazel? How does this story reflect particular manifestations of hope as meaning and in the face of death? What does it suggest about care? How does it relate to our definition? What are some of the possibilities and limits embedded in this story in terms of hope?

In the face of the devastating illness and loss of her son, Pat intuitively seeks out ways to claim meaning in the midst of pain and anguish. She seeks out ways to honor the meaningfulness of her son's life that reflect the distinctiveness of who he was in all his uniqueness. For the boy who loved to climb trees, a big climbing tree is planted on a playground for other children to climb. For the boy who shared freely, toys are given to one who holds a special place for him. For the boy who proudly prayed for God's presence and protection, his mother meditatively needlepoints his prayer from her heart. For the boy who liked to make people feel better, his organs are given that others might have life. In multiple ways, Pat bears witness to the meaningfulness of her son's life and wrestles forth meaningful possibility out of what is otherwise meaningless tragedy. Her actions express her need to have tangible signs of the ways her son's life has made a difference. Among many other things, through her actions, she honors the one who taught her how to love.

Pat recognizes the possibilities for meaningful action even and in spite of the meaninglessness of cancer robbing Nicholas and their family of their future together. The actions of meaning are actions that gesture toward hope even in the midst of devastation. There is drivenness, even desperation, about Pat's need to make meaning that I have seen also with others who have lost children. It is as if life is held together only insofar as meaningful action is remembered, performed, and anticipated. Hope lingers in the balance between.

Pat's actions that honor the particularity of who Nicholas is raise up not only the meaningfulness of his life but also the meaningfulness of all of life. As the precious uniqueness of one much-loved son is honored, so too is the precious gift of all life, each life. How is this so? We see this on a couple of levels. First, in the concrete lives of particular people (kids who will climb the tree, the boy up the street, the organ recipients and their families, and so on), precious lives are honored and even enriched through Nicholas's death. While it is disturbing to say it, it is also true. At another level, as Nicholas's life is raised up as one full of meaning, so the meaningfulness of all of life—both actual and potential—is represented and raised up. When one life is reverenced, all life is reverenced. Hope's possibility is glimpsed as the meaningfulness of life is insisted upon, especially in situations where meaninglessness seems ever present.

There is much in this story that demonstrates the powerful witness of hope as meaning in spite of death, tragedy, and sadness. However, for Pat, it does not stop there. While her need to *make meaning* and bear witness to Nicholas's life through gifts to others is key, it is also sustained by a sense of transcendent presence. Pat described her faith as "more spiritual than religious" but also kept somewhat connected to her local church, where Nicholas was baptized, which they attended on high holidays, and where his funeral was held. Interestingly, unlike many in such times of horrible loss, Pat does not interpret Nicholas's death as part of some larger plan of God or the way things were "meant to be." She does not consider that Nicholas's death is meaningful in and of itself, endowed with some unfathomable transcendent purpose. Rather, Pat gives all of her heart and soul to witnessing to the meaningfulness of his life, as short as it was—a life that she never seems to question is a gift to her and now also to many others. It is Nicholas's life, not his death, that Pat seeks to hold up as having eternal meaning and significance. This is witnessed to powerfully through giving away his organs, giving his toys, planting a tree, and other actions. Though her faith is challenged, the God she believes in and gravitates back to is one who affirms her focused attempts to bring forth meaning out of meaninglessness and honors this eternally. She trusts that her actions are saturated with transcendent meaning which in some way bind her to Nicholas through God, who holds together heaven and earth.

Although Pat, in the face of the tragic loss of her son, struggles at times with the question of the existence of God, she also yearns for God's presence as that which assures her of Nicholas's safety and connects her earthly being with her son's heavenly being. While she wrestles in time with questions of afterlife and whether the meaningfulness of Nicholas's life ends in the giving of his organs and life to others, she also speaks of Nicholas as alive in heaven, happy with the way his life has made others' lives better. In one conversation, she noted, "I know it's crazy, but sometimes I tell God to make sure to give Nicholas a hug for me before bed." Her relationship with God emerges as that which connects her with her son and opens her up to the horizon of eternity.

In the reading of Psalm 139, there is the affirmation of God forming all of life in its uniqueness and the assurance of God's presence in all of life, even in death. In reading these words, the transcendent meaning of life, especially Nicholas's life, is held up with poetry that has been uttered among believers for millennia. So too with the actions of anointing and participation in the Lord's Prayer; words and actions bind the present moment with the communion of saints that have gone before. In no way do these actions lessen the overwhelming pain and tragedy of Nicholas's death. However, in the midst of the agony, these actions open up space for eternity to touch time, for heaven to touch earth, and provide tangible actions that point to intangible possibility.

What can be said of care that affirms hope's presence in such moments of devastation? We can see that care here means supporting Pat in her creative attempts to make meaning in ways that honor and revere the ultimate meaningfulness of life, through the particular life of one child. It means honoring the ways that Nicholas's life has changed her life and that of others. It means holding up the meaning of Nicholas's life, both in time and in eternity, through words and actions that resonate within and beyond the present moment. Holding up hope as meaning in this instance can include supporting her in specific actions that make concrete differences in others' lives,[2] actions that are symbolic and personal,[3] collective ritual actions,[4] and those that mark special days throughout the year. Further, such care can include connecting Pat with her community of faith and with others who have suffered similar loss in order that she might participate in communities of caring and understanding.

In terms of our working definition of hope, we see how specific concrete actions represent the opening up of horizons of meaning and participation through the reverencing of life—both the life of Nicholas and the lives of those who receive life-giving gifts from Nicholas. We can see how Pat's relationship with her son, even in death, helps to mediate relationships with others, with transcendence, and even with time, all of which point to hope's quiet presence. Hope is not present for Pat by anticipation of the future, for the future without Nicholas overwhelms and disorients her. For Pat, the future is conceivable

2. For example, actions such as donating her son's organs and giving away her son's toys.

3. For example, actions such as needlepointing "Nicholas's Prayer," asking God to hug Nicholas

4. For example, ritual actions such as the bedside ritual, the funeral, the tree-planting ceremony, participation in the walk for cancer.

only through planning actions that honor her son. Pat does, however, glimpse hope's possibility when the present is opened to transcendence. While images of Nicholas lying in the cold ground still plague her a few months after his burial, she also carries images of her son playing with friends in heaven and of Nicholas being bathed in light and love. These latter images help Pat to let go and entrust Nicholas to God's care. Meaningful actions that remember and honor her son in life reflect the opening of horizons to eternity where Nicholas exists, signifying in some sense that nothing is ever lost. All is held within a much larger whole.

For Pat, the weight of despair exists simultaneously with hope as meaning. Through this time, there is never a moment when she does not carry the burden of grief in her body and soul. Engaging in meaningful action that honors Nicholas is part of what enables her to continue to breathe, to exist, to stay connected with life. Such actions help her find ways to continue to be in the face of his devastating absence. The anguish she experiences in losing her son points to its opposite—to the fullness of love she has known with Nicholas and the way she has been changed by this. The hope present for Pat is not a high-pitched, obvious hope. Rather, it is hope that breathes quietly beneath and within all actions that point to Nicholas's life, and to all of life, as meaningful and precious, the gift of eternity in time, even in hiddenness.

POSSIBILITIES AND LIMITS

More than anyone else, Viktor Frankl focuses on the intrinsic connections between meaning, hope, and suffering. In his book *Man's Search for Meaning*, Frankl outlines the ways the human "will to meaning" demonstrated through concrete meaningful actions can represent hope even in the most terrible and meaningless of circumstances. In descriptions of his life in a concentration camp, he tells how meaninglessness, misery, and a disconnection from anything but the immediacy of death and the cheapness of life left many in a state of dire hopelessness. He also describes moments in which meaningful actions among prisoners bore witness to the potential for meaning—a "yes" to life despite the spirit of meaninglessness and death that was everywhere present.[5] Affirming the centrality of meaning in life, Frankl quotes Nietzsche: "[One] who has a why

5. Most powerful among Frankl's stories is one of him bearing witness to meaning amid meaninglessness and feeding hope. He recalls being asked to say something to the fellow prisoners after several people had died. Already dying from starvation, the prisoners had given up food for a day rather than tell the Nazis the identity of the prisoner who had stolen some potatoes. At the end of this difficult day, the electricity went off, and they lay in darkness. The senior warden told Frankl to get up and say something to help stop them dying from hopelessness. In his book, he shares what he said in his attempt

to live can bear with almost any how.["6] When one has a sense of purpose and meaning, almost any suffering can be endured and even endowed with purpose and meaning. "Saying 'yes to life in spite of everything,' . . . presupposes that life is potentially meaningful under any conditions, even those which are most miserable.["7]

Later in his life in an interview, Frankl argues that as humans we need to admit our inability and incapacity to recognize the ultimate meaning of our lives in intellectual and rational terms, especially in the face of massive evil. However, we can still believe in ultimate meaning, to which meaningful action attests. Frankl describes despair as suffering without meaning. But the minute one takes a stand against meaninglessness through meaningful action, one can turn tragedy into triumph.[8]

In his autobiographical reflections on meaning, hope, suffering, and the human condition throughout his post-holocaust career, we see the extent to which he himself engages in acts of meaning making by weaving "the slender threads of a broken life into a firm pattern of meaning."[9] We can see the degree to which, in giving voice to the horrors of the concentration camp and building his theory of logotherapy out of this experience, he endows his experience with meaning that opens up hope's possibility in life—in his life and that of others.

While Frankl's reflections on meaning and hope in the face of adversity are powerful and resonate with our present discussion, a couple of his insights need to be highlighted. For Frankl, one makes a decision for meaning, a decision for hope. He sees this decision as a responsibility to claim meaning in spite of all the negations in life. Further, Frankl emphasizes the role of the individual human agency to claim and construct such meaning and hope in life. While he does, at points, suggest that ultimate meaning exists beyond human understanding, his primary emphasis is upon meaning making as an aspect of being for which an individual needs to take responsibility. It is a human responsibility to construct meaning from the multiple fragments of our lives.

With some of Frankl's work and that of others who focus on the importance of meaning making in the production of hope,[10] I have a concern about ethics and what or who is served through practices of meaning making.

"to find a full meaning in our life then and there, in that hut and in that practically hopeless situation." Viktor E. Frankl, *Man's Search for Meaning*, rev. ed. (New York: Washington Square, 1984), 105.

6. Frankl, quoting Nietzsche, in *Man's Search for Meaning*, 97.

7. Frankl, "The Case for a Tragic Optimism," in *Man's Search for Meaning*, 161–62.

8. Interview, South Africa, 1985 (Part I, Part II, and Part III). Victor Frankl Institut. http://logotherapy.univie.ac.at/e/clipgallery.html

9. Gordon W. Allport, preface to Frankl, *Man's Search for Meaning*, 9.

It is not a given that acts of meaning making in themselves will inevitably serve good ends. Even hope as meaning can be misconstrued to serve destructive ends. As an example, I can imagine any number of dictators in the world right now engaging in acts of so-called meaning making and even considering such acts as a means to feed their hope for a certain outcome. However, if that outcome is destructive of life, love, and goodness, can we really affirm such meaning making in the production of hope? Clearly not. Instead, it must be understood that acts of meaning making in relation to hope stand over and against meaninglessness in all its guises. To affirm that life in all its particularity is meaningful in the face of all that suggests otherwise is an act of defiance that gives direction and substance to acts of meaning making that actually manifest hope. While I do not believe Frankl would disagree with this concern, I want to hold it up as a caution.

Further, while it is important to affirm acts of meaning making over against meaninglessness, it also is important to consider how such acts are generative in the lives of others and also point to larger transcendent meaning. In the first instance, we can see how acts that affirm meaningfulness generate meaning in the lives of others. In Nicholas's story, we see this in the many ways his mother's acts of meaning making generate meaning in other people's lives. Second, people of faith are also challenged to see how such acts point to the fullness of meaning found ultimately in God. Though the human creation of meaning is important for hope, ultimately hope does not exist in the human creation of meaning. Rather, meaning making that manifests hope is reflexive, both embodying and pointing beyond specific acts to an ultimate meaning that both transcends and is manifested in all acts of meaning. One way to consider this distinction is to explore the following question: In our efforts to make meaning, are humans the creators of meaning, or do human acts of meaning making reflect a fullness of meaning that is given, that comes from God? While for people of faith, the answer may well be "Both are true," it is helpful to see the distinction here.

This concept of hope as meaning being generative and as pointing beyond to transcendence is well demonstrated in the following practice. In urban-center hospital ERs, it is not uncommon for people to die without anyone present and without anyone even knowing the deceased person's name. At one hospital, it became common practice that when someone had died and the

---

10. See descriptions of spirituality, hope, and meaning making in the health care literature in Pam McCarroll, Thomas St. James O'Connor, and Elizabeth Meakes, "Assessing Plurality in Spirituality Definitions," in *Spirituality and Health: Multidisciplinary Explorations*, ed. Augustine Meier, Thomas St. James O'Connor, and Peter Van Katwyk (Waterloo: Wilfred Laurier University Press, 2005), 40–43.

identity and next of kin were unknown, the hospital chaplain would enact a ritual. It was a ritual of blessing (or "honoring," as it is known in secular hospital settings) to reverence the person's life and to mark the meaningfulness of life in all its particularity. Sometimes the chaplain was alone with the unnamed person—the John or Jane Doe. Sometimes other health care workers joined in. The person's face was uncovered, and a hand of blessing was held above the forehead. Words to reverence the gift of life were uttered, and a moment of silence was held to remember the sanctity of life as it had been manifested in this one person. In the context of the ER, where the frantic busyness of trauma can sometimes cheapen life, such acts are reminders of the transcendent sanctity, meaning, and gift of life and proved to be generative of meaning for hospital staff. The mere enacting of this ritual generated and honored hope as meaning, both finite and transcendent.

Another area for further consideration is the role of the individual and the role of the community in the understanding of hope as meaning. Frankl's work focuses primarily on individuals forging meaning and not so much on the role and responsibility of communities to construct meaning. While the importance of hope as meaning and the role of individual responsibility to claim meaning is well demonstrated by Frankl (and by our story of Pat and Nicholas), something is missing if we do not highlight the importance of hope as meaning created and narrated in community. It is often through shared narratives and the ways people discover themselves participating in such shared narratives that hope as meaning is opened up.

The Jewish and Christian Scriptures attest to the importance of hope as meaning as it is constructed and narrated in community. When life is experienced in the extremity of loss, violence, dislocation, and oppression, the Jews of the Hebrew Scriptures remember and retell the stories of the past saving work of God, who redeemed them from adversity. Remembering the ways God saved their ancestors in the past—from the oppression in Egypt, for example—relocates the present moment of suffering into a larger narrative of redemption within which they participate. Meaning and hope are opened up through reframing their present experience of trial and suffering into a larger story. By telling the story of the past, they relocate the present, anticipating God's saving work in history. In the collective recollection of the larger narrative of God's people, those who presently suffer are relocated within a larger narrative that yearns toward a promised future—a future that is *remembered* in the stories of God's saving acts that have gone before. In terms of hope as meaning, the role of community and the shared narratives of communities in relation to God are central. Hope is known in the dynamic interaction between the community and God and the ways this story is shared and narrated in the present.

Another important area for consideration in our discussion of hope as meaning was intimated in our reflection on the case of Nicholas and Pat. It revolves around the common way many interpret sudden adversity as "God's will" or the secular version of the same idea expressed in the common refrain "It was meant to be." Such interpretations of adverse events also point to hope as meaning. The suggestion is that God or the universe is in control, so everything that happens is part of some transcendent plan. There is inevitability about it. The movement toward hope as meaning here comes through obedience or consent to this higher power. Indeed, for many Christians, the Jesus narrative is understood in these terms; Jesus' death is part of God's plan that serves the greater plan of redemption through resurrection. Read into contemporary experiences of suffering, such embedded theology interprets that whatever happens is endowed with meaning by the sheer fact that "it was meant to be" or "it was God's plan." While the experience of the event as meaningful may be inexplicable to the human mind and heart—as in the case of a happy six-year-old boy dying suddenly from cancer—the assumption is that it has meaning in the larger scheme of things. One may not be able to perceive the meaning, but it is presumed to be meaningful nonetheless. Thus, suffering itself is given meaning and even seen to be redemptive in and of itself within a larger (often imperceptible) plan.

For some who believe such conceptions of God or the universe, events of acute pain can cause them to fight and turn bitter and resentful against life and whatever power they perceive to control life. The pain they experience is too much for their faith or system of belief to bear. For others, however, acceptance of the will of this higher power can be a means of acceptance and a pathway to hope. While I myself cannot hold to such conceptions of God as one in control who wields power this way, even though it is a common way to interpret God's power and the narrative of Jesus' death and resurrection, I have experienced the grace and hope that can emerge in such expressions of faith. When I was present upon the sudden death of a Muslim man, the agony and grief of a wife and daughter were visibly lifted by the imam's reminder: "It was his time to go. Allah (peace be upon him) had ordained it before he was born, before you even laid eyes on him. There was nothing you could have done to change it. There is nothing he could have done to change it." The sense of release, of grace and even hope that broke forth in the room as these words were uttered was palpable. Mother and daughter were freed from the frantic what-ifs, relieved from the burden of the present, and opened to accept the gift of their loved one's life and to the larger reality in which God was the author. They need not worry but could rest in the assurance of God.

Indeed, for early and contemporary followers of Christ, the ways meaning and hope are related in contexts of suffering and adversity has everything to do with the ways the story of Jesus' humiliation, torture, death, and resurrection is understood and lived. For most Christians, not only does the interpretation of this story manifest embedded theology regarding all the major doctrines,[11] but also this story is read into experiences of suffering and adversity in life. How this narrative interprets adverse events frames the understanding of hope as meaning as it is lived out.

From the perspective of post-resurrection communities, the stories of Jesus' humiliation, torture, and death carry an abundance of meaning that cannot be given voice easily or neatly. Whether crucifixion is seen as a means to the end goal of resurrection or whether resurrection is seen primarily as the vindication of the fullness of meaning present in the crucifixion is central to how hope as meaning in contexts of suffering is read into life. In the tradition of the theology of the cross, I tend to the latter perspective. The suffering and death of Jesus paradoxically embodies the dashed hopes of those who sought God's reign through a powerful Messiah and the hidden hope that refuses to return power for power; the dashed hope of a just world and the hidden hope of divine solidarity with all those who suffer injustice; the dashed hope of happy endings and the hidden hope that even in the face of the worst assaults of evil, love remains, and love's power brings forth new life and impossible possibilities. For a postresurrection people, all these and more dashed and hidden hopes hang upon the cross in Jesus, vindicated absolutely in resurrection.

God did not arrange for Nicholas to have cancer and to die at six years of age. It was not in God's plan that this should happen. But God was present in the community of love gathered around that insisted on the precious meaning of Nicholas's life. God was present in the will to claim meaning and to reverence and honor life as love had revealed it and made it known in Nicholas. God was present in solidarity with Nicholas and Pat within the meaningless chance of cancer destroying lives. And God is present now, holding the promise of new life in this world and the next.

---

11. The major doctrines I refer to here include doctrines of God, Jesus' person and work, doctrines of creation and redemption and understandings of suffering, injustice and evil and so on.

CONCLUSION

When the pull to meaninglessness overwhelms, what does hope-enabling care look like? In such situations, practices of care exist primarily in embodying meaningful caring relationships and supporting people to discern and claim the meaning and meaningfulness of life despite all that presses toward meaninglessness. Such care often includes hearing a person's story and bearing witness to the meaningfulness of this life lived, for better and for worse. In the latter case, co-constructing ways to address the negative residue from the past is an important process by which to open up hope and to embody the reality that life matters and that all action and inaction matter. Practices of care in this case include facilitating people to make links between micro and macro levels of meaning, links between the particularity of a person's life and larger narratives of meaning. This may be done by linking particular human stories with scriptural or other narratives that point to larger horizons within which their story resonates and connects. It may include reframing interpreted meanings of life stories in ways that feed connectedness with others, with time, with creation and the transcendent. Care practices in this case are mindful to resist the pull to meaninglessness and to support people to participate in actions and thought that reverence life in all its forms. Such action and thought affirm the absolute and transcendent meaning of life held within a wholeness and purpose beyond what the eye can see. Further, such practices of care can include the co-creation of rituals to represent meaning that transcends verbal, word constructions and find resonance in other aspects of embodiment—in sight, touch, sound, smell, taste. Rituals can be important ways to mark transitions in life and to affirm transcendent meaning beyond what words can express. Rituals both manifest meaningful action and point beyond the ritual itself to meaning that transcends and enfolds all that is.

Life can be brutal, and it is easy to fall into a pit of meaninglessness. However, our discussion on hope as meaning demonstrates the extent to which acts of meaning making not only stand defiant against the pull toward meaninglessness, but also are generative of meaning in the self and others and bear witness to the meaningfulness of life as a whole that transcends time and space. Our discussion points to the importance of community in generating hope as meaning in the shared narratives within which we participate. It has examined diverse ways transcendent meaning may be perceived in the face of suffering and adversity and how such perceptions affect the way we interpret hope as meaning in life. Through our treatment of the narrative of cross and resurrection, we perceive the extent to which, for Christians, this story forms our sense of hope as meaning in contexts of suffering and adversity. All of these explorations of hope as meaning point to ways that present experiences of adversity and suffering are opened up to larger horizons—in relationship with others, with time, and with the transcendent—that enable humans to experience themselves participating in a larger whole. While our discussion of hope as meaning overlaps in some ways with our discussion of hope as fight, neither option, even when thought through together, exhausts hope's manifestation in life.

5

Hope as Survival

But Sarah saw the son of Hagar the Egyptian, whom she had borne to Abraham, playing with her son Isaac. So she said to Abraham, "Cast out this slave woman with her son; for the son of this slave woman shall not inherit along with my son Isaac." . . . So Abraham rose early in the morning, and took bread and a skin of water, and gave it to Hagar, putting it on her shoulder, along with the child, and sent her away. And she departed, and wandered about in the wilderness of Beer-sheba.

When the water in the skin was gone, she cast the child under one of the bushes. Then she went and sat down opposite him a good way off, about the distance of a bowshot; for she said, "Do not let me look on the death of the child." And as she sat opposite him, she lifted up her voice and wept. And God heard the voice of the boy; and the angel of God called to Hagar from heaven, and said to her, "What troubles you, Hagar? Do not be afraid; for God has heard the voice of the boy where he is. Come, lift up the boy and hold him fast with your hand, for I will make a great nation of him." Then God opened her eyes and she saw a well of water. She went, and filled the skin with water, and gave the boy a drink.
Gen. 21:9-10, 14-21

The abuse had started when Jacqui[1] was young. First it was physical and emotional. Then, once she entered puberty at ten years of age, her father and uncle started to sexually abuse her. She didn't know what to do; they

---

1. The story of Jacqui is based on true stories of women I have worked with and known professionally and personally who have survived abuse. Jacqui's story is the result of combining several people's stories to ensure the confidentiality of all. Names, location, details, and timing have been altered to ensure further confidentiality. The person generally represented in the street chaplain ("Linda") has reviewed and provided input on this chapter.

were so much bigger than she was, and no one would believe her anyway. Jacqui once tried to talk to her mother, but her mom was usually too drunk or depressed to do anything. So Jacqui would stay away, sleep over at friends' homes, and try to be elsewhere when she knew that either of the men was around. Jacqui remembers that when it did happen, she would lose touch with life, just disappearing into a different world. She also started cutting herself whenever she felt the sick, shameful feeling surge within her.

After several years, she knew she had to get out. She left her home and took a bus to the big city, where she found a youth shelter. Jacqui liked the youth shelter at first. She made some friends—others who were running from a lot of bad stuff, too, all of them just trying to have a normal life. It wasn't long before she got into a relationship with Joe, a man she had met at the bus station when she arrived. It was like he was waiting for her. He was funny and nice. He knew his way around the city and promised to take care of her. At first, their relationship seemed good. They partied together. She met other people. But soon he wanted her to contribute to the rent and pay for her own food, clothes and entertainment by doing tricks with other guys for money. He had her "practice" with his friends, and soon, before she could realize what was happening, he became her pimp. The drugs had started by then. More drugs meant more tricks and it became a bad cycle.

One night, Joe beat her up after she returned home without enough money for his next fix. This time, Jacqui left. Bruised and still a little high, she ran into Linda, the street chaplain. This was when their relationship really began. They'd met a few weeks before, when Linda had given her an outreach bag. Now when they met, Jacqui shared what had happened. After hearing her story, Linda arranged for her to get to a safe house, where she could hide from Joe, get some sleep, and try to figure out her next steps. Eventually, Jacqui started back to school, taking classes for her high school diploma. With Linda's help, she even found transitional housing and got linked into the employment programs available. Over the next few years, things started to get a bit better.

But then Jacqui hit a wall. A job prospect fell through, and she couldn't find work. In her desperation, she had a few one-night stands, which made her feel shameful and mad at herself and triggered flashbacks and dissociative episodes. The flashbacks intruded into her nights and threw her days into confused turmoil. She started cutting her skin again and found herself back into drugs. This time, the drugs were the over-the-counter variety. She stayed somewhat connected with Linda, who said that, whenever she was ready, she could help Jacqui find a group and support to help her. But starting from scratch again? It felt like too much for Jacqui. Just before taking the full bottle of pills, she sent Linda a quick text that said, "Good-bye. It's not your fault. It's just all too much." Jacqui was found unconscious on the floor of her apartment. Linda made the 911 call, accompanied her to the hospital, sat with her among the life-saving machines, contacted her family, and called on all friends and colleagues to pray, feverishly. So we did.

With the letters H-O-P-E permanently scarred on her thigh, Jacqui lay hovering between life and death for many hours. After a few days, she recovered enough to be discharged and referred to a shelter to await housing in a different part of the city and to a community-based trauma recovery program. By Jacqui's own admission, a trauma recovery program was not what she wanted to do, but she promised Linda that she would give it a try. Remembering all that she had lived in her twenty-nine years was hard. But doing it with others who had also suffered abuse made it a little easier to bear. There were fits and starts, moments when it all felt too much, when the flashbacks came, when she broke down, unable to speak, slouched on the floor, weeping and dazed, fragments of memories cutting in and out.

In group therapy, Jacqui learned about the trauma of sexual violence and the experiences common among survivors. She discovered the difference between living as a "victim" and living as a "survivor." When she heard others' stories of survival, she began to imagine the possibility of healing for herself. She developed techniques that helped her feel safe and grounded when things started to go crazy within. She figured out how to take care of herself and how important it was to have some trusted people in her life. The group learning and sharing process was important for Jacqui on many fronts. However, what really began to make life seem livable was digging her hands into clay and telling through sculpted pottery the story of her past and her hopes for the future.

The sculpture Jacqui created in the art therapy group represented hope for her. It carried the burden of her past within a larger picture of her life and sense of possibility. The sculpture is best viewed by looking down at it on a table. A large rectangular base frames the contrasting halves of her sculpture, representing the contrasting parts of her life. Half of it is darkly colored with jagged edges. Splayed remnants of a nest are torn and scattered across the sculpted surface. Fragile eggs are crushed and broken open, oozing blood-colored yolks. A small, weak sculpted bird cowers in a dark corner, barely visible unless pointed out. The other half of the sculpture transitions into lively, vivid colors and undulating shapes. In the center sits a sturdy grass-made nest full of brightly colored eggs. Two of the eggs are being cracked open from the life stirring within them, ready to come into the world. A magenta, orange, and turquoise patterned bird leans over the eggs, seeming to tend and care for them.

In the corner is a sapling tree with leaves sprouting on its branches and with butterflies and bugs crawling on it. Grass and flowers grow all around.

Jacqui described the process of making the sculpture. She started by making the brightly colored bird, which she now calls Mama Bird. She decorated Mama Bird with her favorite wildly contrasting colors. Only after making her bird did she begin to create the dark side of her sculpture, with Mama Bird standing and watching alongside. When she made the little bird cowering in the corner, Jacqui was aware that she was portraying herself as a child and teen with all the terror, loneliness, fragility, and darkness of life, inside and out, at that time. Only when she began creating the brightly colored side, after neatly forming her nest and sculpting her eggs, did Jacqui realize that Mama Bird also was a portrayal of her. Mama Bird was Jacqui now as she was trying to image herself—beautiful, resilient, and full of life. She needed to bring Mama Bird into being before she could begin to do all the work required for the dark side of her life to be portrayed. When she realized this, she placed a tiny, mutely colored orange, magenta, and turquoise dot under the turned-down beak of the tiny wounded bird—a reminder that beauty can emerge from the worst of all situations. She also placed small patterns of her small, wounded bird across the breast of Mama Bird. She carries herself—small, wounded bird—with her as Mama Bird. In contrast to the experience of her past, when life's possibility was crushed and only violence, loneliness, fear, and darkness seemed to prevail, now she seeks to focus on the new life that has begun to come forth from within her. Unlike the crushed eggs of her past, her yearning for new life is represented in the colorful eggs being cracked open from the life bursting forth within.

This time, Jacqui tells Linda, she will stick with it – she will stick with life. She knows life will be hard at times, but if she keeps doing her art and seeing people she can trust, things will get better, little by little. She knows she will be hit again by the harshness of what she has lived. But she also knows now what she needs to do when she feels herself falling into the disconnected numbness of dissociation or senses a flashback coming on. She gently grasps and rubs the small sculpted egg she carries around in her pocket. Her well-developed awareness enables her to recognize what's going on, and she is able to redirect herself to a safe place. Jacqui now recognizes that she needs to stay away from certain areas and people. When the self-hatred starts to creep up on her, she enacts the self-soothing exercises she created with her therapy group. Most of all, Jacqui has safe people to call upon if life gets really tough.

REFLECTING WITH JACQUI

How is hope present in the story of Jacqui? How does this story reflect particular manifestations of hope as survival and in the face of trauma? What does it suggest about care? How does it relate to our definition? What are some of the possibilities and limits embedded in this story in terms of hope?

If you ask Jacqui now, she would describe herself as a survivor—a survivor of repeated sexual abuse and violence in her family, in her intimate relationships, and on the streets; a survivor of emotional and physical abuse; a survivor of parents and a community raised in a residential school, robbed of so much; and a survivor of multiple attempts at suicide. The image of survivor has become an important one for Jacqui in her journey to reclaim herself in a way that acknowledges her past but does not allow it to determine who she is. Like many who have participated in therapeutic processes for trauma recovery, the shift from being a "victim" to a "survivor" has been an important part of Jacqui's journey. To claim herself as a survivor has enabled Jacqui to acknowledge that the encounters with death through abuse that have torn into her body and soul have affected her, and there is no pretending otherwise. At the same time, being a survivor means that while she has been marked by the trauma of her past, she is not possessed by it. She has survived multiple encounters with the very real threat of death and lives to tell the tale. Jacqui has been marked by trauma, but she has not been claimed by it and courageously claims it as part—but not all—of her story.

If you ask her about the H-O-P-E carved into her leg, she'll tell you that story, too—about the time when she woke up despairing that she was still alive. Cutting into her thigh was a way to release the pain inside, to get it into her flesh rather than swirling madly within her. At the time, the word meant only that—the hope that pain in her flesh could give her a focus and some relief from the inner demons that plagued her in that moment. She did not really think about the fact that it would scar and still be readable years later. Now she looks at the scar as a kind of mark of truth, a mark that makes a connection between surviving death and the possibility for life—HOPE. She survived. She survived many moments when life seemed impossible, unlivable, sheer suffering and misery.

For Jacqui, hope does not exist in some idealized future, though she does dream sometimes. For her, hope emerges from the reality that despite all she has lived through, she survives. Even when memories surge forth and threaten to overpower her in the present, drawing her back into reliving the past, she finds her way by reclaiming herself as a survivor of these events, locating them in the past and grounding herself in relation to the present. She knows that she will always live with her well-practiced patterns of self-protection and reactivity developed to survive the trauma. But she also has begun to develop new patterns of response that help her body and mind remember that she is not doomed to reenact the trauma of her past. To be a survivor means that what one has survived—the encounter with the powers of death and destruction—is in the past. The shift toward hope in this instance is the recognition that, because she is a survivor, horizons have opened up that were never expected to open up. What had been thought of as impossibility—survival—has become possibility. And while some survivors carry survival as a kind of burden, it also holds within it a breath of hope that remains.

Jacqui's sculpture represented a turning point for her where the full story could begin to be portrayed.[2] In terms of our definition of hope, we can see how horizons of meaning and participation opened up for her as she sought to put the pieces of life together in sculpted form. Creating the sculpture was sometimes gut-wrenching. She would find herself in tears, mourning for the teenage Jacqui who was so broken, despairing, wounded, and filled with shame. Other times she needed to throw the clay at the wall and pound it down, releasing rage that what had happened to her could happen to her, to anyone at all. She spoke about how important it was to feel the clay and shape it with her hands. Forming representations of parts of her life that were so dark and overwhelming helped her feel more released on the inside. She did not need to live in fear and terror as she had. Creating the bright and colorful scene helped to give form and shape to the possibility for newness. As she sculpted Mama Bird, the nest, and the eggs, it was as if a parallel process was going on within her—honoring her colorful and resilient self, creating a safe sense of home, and bringing forth the new life that was fragile but emerging into the world. Hope's horizons open for Jacqui in relation to her own story in time, in relation to other people, and in feeling reconnected with life.

2. The Barbra Shlifer Clinic in Toronto, Ontario, has many programs similar to the one described in Jacqui's story. An art show, *Transformation by Fire*, was held at the Gardiner Museum of Ceramic Art from February 7 to April 23, 2013. This show included the ceramic work of many women survivors of violence enrolled in the art therapy program at the Shlifer Clinic. In the online video, one woman describes her experience of sculpting in these words: "We made a sculpture called rebuilding your home. I built a little world made of houses and children playing. I tried to show both the innocence of children and that it happens around the world that children are harmed. When we burned the sculpture . . . it broke into a million pieces in the process of burning. It became a parallel to my life because I actually enjoyed putting it back together. I would like to encourage anyone who has survived something terrible, being a survivor of violence, 'Don't give up, and if you can, find a way to be creative.'" "Gardiner Expressive Arts Group," Tumblr, February 5, 2013, http://gardinerexpressiveartsgroup.tumblr.com/post/42369143738/video-hope-transformationbyfire-women.

Care for Jacqui has meant many things. Education about trauma and recovery in a group setting was important because it helped her to realize that she was not alone or isolated. Not only had others in the group experienced some similar kinds of trauma, but there was a whole theory that helped her understand what had happened to her because of the trauma. For Jacqui, an important part of the process was her increasing recognition of her own body's cues when the trauma memories were getting the upper hand. She developed tools and techniques for dealing with these moments and honed grounding and self-soothing habits. Most importantly, care for Jacqui meant safe space and people with whom to share and express her story—in words, tears, gasps, and art. In the literature, such care is often described as bearing witness to the testimony of the other.[3] Indeed, for Jacqui, a few people became safe places for her to express her story, a handful of people who bore witness to her testimony. As well, there were those who cared for her by holding hope for her on her behalf. When she was caught in the pit, Linda and the other therapists were there, holding forth hope for Jacqui when she could see no hope, nothing of goodness and beauty, in herself or in life.

Jacqui's story is far from over. She carries both vulnerability and possibility within her. As she continues her efforts to heal, there may come a time when she more fully explores the cycle of violence that her parents were caught up in and the embodied trauma of survivors of the residential school system. There may come a time when she wants to confront her parents and uncle with the reality of what has happened. There may come a time when she can forgive herself and others at a deeper level. There may come a time when learning about and claiming the history, spirituality, and spiritual practices of her aboriginal ancestors becomes a healing movement in her life. While she has begun to participate in the yearly women's march to take back the streets, there may come a time when she wants to more fully invest herself in advocacy and social justice on behalf of women survivors of violence—or maybe not. One way or another, hope exists at this moment in her as one who has survived. The horizons of possibility have opened up unexpectedly, and a new perspective on her life has become possible.

3. Shelly Rambo, *Spirit and Trauma: A Theology of Remaining* (Louisville: Westminster John Knox, 2010), 16, 23–24, 38. Many thinkers and practitioners argue for the importance of bearing witness and giving testimony; among them are Elie Wiesel, Arthur Frank, Judith Herman, and John Swinton, to name a few.

Possibilities and Limits

The use of the term *survivor* in the North American context has been expanding exponentially over the last decade or so. We hear the language of survivor now used frequently in relation to illness, especially cancer: "I am a breast cancer survivor." We hear it in relation to great and to lesser, tongue-in-cheek feats of endurance: "I survived Mount Kilimanjaro"; "I survived frosh week." We even have a top-grossing TV program called *Survivor*. And, of course, as with Jacqui's story, we hear survivor discourse in relation to much-publicized stories of survival of sexual abuse—survivors of the abuse of team coaches, priests, and the residential school system, to name a few. There is a marked surge in the use of survivor discourse in the public realm, and within that, there are several important distinctions to be made related to our discussion of hope as survival.

In considering hope as survival through Jacqui's story, it is clear that the primary background literature related to her therapy revolves around trauma theory, especially the quickly growing field related to the trauma of sexual violence. Research in the larger field of trauma studies includes a focus on post-traumatic stress (PTS) among survivors of war, torture, kidnapping, natural disasters, and so on. Recent work in the field has begun to explore the extent to which protective patterns in the brain and body memory, initially helpful in surviving extreme trauma, can become inhibitors to healing, requiring re-patterning of brain and body pathways. We sense how important this process of re-patterning was in Jacqui's healing.

Robert J. Lifton's groundbreaking work with survivors of psychological trauma in war describes a survivor as "one who has encountered, been exposed to, or witnessed death and has himself or herself remained alive."[4] Judith Herman builds on Lifton's work and seeks to break down the division between the so-called public and private realms that keep the trauma of sexual violence hidden from view. She describes survivors as those who have experienced an encounter with death as a threat so overpowering that the normal adaptive systems are overwhelmed and unable to function.[5] Such events—especially if there is no ability to escape, if they are repeated, and if they happen in childhood or adolescence—compound a sense of helplessness that leads to a heightened post-traumatic stress response. Psychological trauma of this sort refuses to be

---

4. Robert J. Lifton, "The Concept of the Survivor," in *The Future of Immortality and Other Essays for a Nuclear Age* (New York: Basic, 1987), 235. See University of California Television, "Conversations with History: Robert J. Lifton," October 29, 2001, available on YouTube at http://www.youtube.com/watch?v=vEn1KuE5De0.

5. Judith Herman, *Trauma and Recovery: The Aftermath of Violence—from Domestic Abuse to Political Terror* (New York: Basic, 1997), 33.

buried. And while there is usually a powerful desire to deny the traumatic event, there "is the conviction that denial does not work."[6]

Herman argues that "remembering and telling the truth about terrible events are prerequisites both for the restoration of the social order and for the healing of individual victims. The conflict between the will to deny horrible events and the will to proclaim them aloud is the central dialectic of psychological trauma."[7] Indeed, denial of the events themselves is considered to be a self-protective response that enables life to continue. However, when denial persists, so do the symptoms of hyperarousal, intrusion (flashbacks), and constriction (disassociation).[8] These symptoms involve the reenactment of past trauma in the present such that the past trauma possesses and takes over present reality. Shelly Rambo argues that the central problem with trauma is temporal:

> The past does not stay, so to speak, in the past. Instead it invades the present, returning in such a way that the present becomes not only an enactment of the past but an enactment about what was not fully known or grasped. The fact that the event was not fully integrated at the time means that something of the event returns at a later time. Its unintegrated nature makes it difficult to locate the suffering in any one place and time.[9]

I have heard survivors describe the feeling of being caught in a prison with no way out. Their lives might be stable for a while, but then something happens, and they find themselves flashing back to the abuse. The mind and body get caught up in a crazy pit of terror and sensation, with no way out. Some have described that during the times when flashbacks and dissociative numbing are particularly dominant, they begin to feel like enemies to themselves.

While there has been much reworking of Herman's theory, the general pattern continues to be a model for many trauma recovery programs. First, safety must be established. This is true in any recovery therapy group or relationship, but it is also true that the survivor must develop the means and capacity to make herself safe. As well, the survivor must be "the author and

6. Ibid., Kindle edition, Kindle locations 44–45.

7. Ibid., Kindle locations 46–47.

8. Ibid., Kindle locations 485–86 : "Hyperarousal reflects the persistent expectation of danger; intrusion reflects the indelible imprint of the traumatic moment; constriction reflects the numbing response of surrender."

9. Rambo, *Spirit and Trauma*, 19.

arbiter of her own recovery."[10] Second, there is a focus on remembrance of the event(s) and mourning for all that this loss has meant for the survivor. How this is remembered and mourned is an area of much discussion in the literature. For some, Herman's emphasis on bringing to mind and to words the memories of trauma has caused a kind of retraumatization and a further reenacting of the power dynamic between abuser and abused in a recovery group or individual therapy. Creative arts therapies have been found to be more effective for many in bringing to expression the memories and the mourning and in helping to find ways to integrate traumatic events into a person's life story while minimizing the possibility for retraumatization. Third, survivors in recovery find ways to reconnect to life—to themselves, to others, to creation, to the transcendent—in ways that feed a healthy trust: "The core experiences of psychological trauma are disempowerment and disconnection from others. Recovery, therefore, is based upon the empowerment of the survivor and the creation of new connections. Recovery can take place only within the context of relationships; it cannot occur in isolation."[11] Fourth, for many it is helpful to engage in missional activities that speak out and advocate for change through social justice initiatives. In this fourth step, we see the extent to which survivors are invited to rechannel the trauma experience into meaningful action that serves a greater good.

As we can see, the theory and practice of recovery for survivors of trauma includes elements of hope as fight, as meaning,[12] and even as lament,[13] while

10. Herman, *Trauma and Recovery*, Kindle locations 1791–92.

11. Ibid., Kindle locations 1788–89.

12. Herman makes the link with the importance of meaning in recovery: "The belief in a meaningful world is formed in relation to others and begins in earliest life. Basic trust, acquired in the primary intimate relationship, is the foundation of faith. Later elaborations of the sense of law, justice, and fairness are developed in childhood in relation to both caretakers and peers. More abstract questions of the order of the world, the individual's place in the community, and the human place in the natural order are normal preoccupations of adolescence and adult development. Resolution of these questions of meaning requires the engagement of the individual with the wider community. Traumatic events, once again, shatter the sense of connection between individual and community, creating a crisis of faith. Lifton found pervasive distrust of community and the sense of a 'counterfeit' world to be common reactions in the aftermath of disaster and war." Ibid., Kindle locations 746–51. Viktor Frankl makes explicit the link between survival and meaning: "To live is to suffer. To survive is to find meaning in the suffering." Frankl, *Man's Search for Meaning*, 11.

13. The importance of mourning what has been lost because of the trauma experience is a central aspect of healing. Some work has been done on the importance of lament, especially communal lament in the tradition of the Psalms, in the healing work of survivors of trauma. For example, see Deborah van Deusen Hunsinger, "Bearing the Unbearable: Trauma, Gospel and Pastoral Care," *Theology Today* 68, no. 1 (2011): 21–22.

also embodying hope as survival. From Jacqui's story, we can see her survival (and her identity as a survivor) as a central axis of hope from which extend the fights for existence, for a positive self-concept, for meaning making, and for meaningful action. In terms of our definition, in claiming herself as a survivor not a victim, Jacqui opens up horizons of meaning and participation. She is one who has survived unexpectedly and begins to receive this survival as a gift and identifying mark. A primary aspect of this recovery process is the extent to which survival itself is reframed as an act of resilience and fight, especially in contexts where survivors have been unable to resist or fight against their abuser at the time. The ongoing existence of the survivor stands as a sign and symbol of a fight to live. Moving into the therapeutic process includes, among other things, elements of resistance against the internalization of the abuser's concept of the self and the fight for healthy self-concept, represented in the movement from victim to survivor. It includes actions that seek to make meaning of past trauma by weaving it into a larger narrative, and it includes actions that seek to make a meaningful difference in the lives of others.

While the trauma recovery process is an important embodiment of hope as survival and links with hope as fight, meaning, and lament, I also want to explore some cautions and alternative perspectives. Arthur Frank in his book *The Wounded Storyteller* discusses the tendency for certain narrative plot lines to colonize the stories we tell, allowing us to speak in certain trajectories but not in others.[14] In considering hope as survival through the lens of trauma recovery, there could be a tendency toward such narrative colonization, a limiting of the possibilities for recognizing the ways hope is present or glimpsed in other experiences of survival.

A commonplace use of survival language that may help us differently understand hope as survival can be seen in the following example. When one asks another how she or he is doing and the person responds, "Oh, I'm surviving," depending on the circumstance, one does not necessarily hear the resilient voice of the survivor in the response. Rather, in common daily circumstances, such a response suggests a sense of defeat or surrender to life's challenges.[15] Rather than thriving, this response indicates, the person is *just* surviving, *just* existing. Shouldn't life be more about thriving, not just surviving? Isn't hope found more in thriving than in surviving?

14. Arthur W. Frank, *The Wounded Storyteller: Body, Illness, and Ethics* (Chicago: University of Chicago Press, 1995), 10–12.

15. When this response, "I am surviving," is given in the context of a shared knowledge of the person living through adversity of some sort, it does carry the intimation of resilience and fortitude.

In a paradoxical way, the language of survival points to the possibility of both life and death as unexpected. At some point, perhaps at multiple points, continued existence was experienced as an impossibility. Survival means that the life that survives is not a given; an unexpected outcome has occurred. At the same time, the language of survival points, in a hidden way, to a sense of shock and terror in the experience of death. In living past the absolute threat of destruction and death, the survivor not only bears witness to hope but also carries the marks of the encounter with the powers of death. Both life and death are manifested bodily, psychologically, and spiritually.

The story of Hagar, quoted at the beginning of the chapter, points to this paradoxical moment and reality in Hagar's survival. This story of survival in the desert has been a powerful narrative for African American women struggling with what it means to hope in their contexts of persecution. In her book, *Sisters in the Wilderness*, Delores Williams tracks Hagar's story of slavery, forced single motherhood, racism, isolation, sexual exploitation, banishment, and her survival with her son, Ishmael. The two of them survive all the weight of oppression thrown at them. They survive past the very real threat of spiritual, psychological, and bodily death. They come to the point where Hagar knows death is imminent and cries out, only to be saved from watching her son die as she sits by helplessly watching. She cannot even fathom any other outcome but death. The future is incomprehensible. Her survival past the terrors of oppression and death comes only as divine possibility, not her own possibility. Yet in Hagar's story, her survival itself is held up as a sign of God's impossible possibility manifested in human existence and resilience, scars and all. So, too, for African American women survivors of systematic violence for generations, who have turned to Hagar's story for solace and inspiration. Their survival itself represents hope—the sign and promise of God's presence even amid the wounds that are carried.

What happens when surviving is experienced primarily as a burden and torment, when the powers of death seem to have the upper hand? What happens when the ending and destruction of something good is far more present in what survives than the possibility for something new? What does survival actually indicate? Inspired by the work of Jonathan Lear, Rambo suggests that survival is that middle place between ending and something else: "The term survival captures something of the suspension of life in the aftermath of a traumatic event. The event becomes the defining event beyond which little can be conceived. Life takes on a fundamentally different definition and the tentative and vulnerable quality of life in the aftermath means that it is life always mixed with death."[16] Survival indicates that one is overliving or living on. Life has exceeded itself.[17] The survivor stands as a "witness between radical ending and impossible beginning."[18] In some sense, "new fields of possibilities emerge not because there are grounds for hope but because there are not."[19] Following trauma, there is an emptiness, a silence, that exists in surviving. No words can speak; no sense remains. Time is suspended in the in-between of what has been and having survived it. The future is incomprehensible.

At the center of the Christian faith stands the story of the torture and execution of the one called Savior. In Jesus, all the hopes and dreams for the Messiah are crushed through the violence of power unleashed upon him. In the face of massive abuse, Jesus is helpless. His flesh is torn, his mind is tormented, his body breaks. The unspeakable happens, and his followers scatter in terror. They are survivors, who as Lifton says, "have encountered, been exposed to, [and] witnessed death and have themselves remained alive." They have experienced helplessness in the face of the powers of death. They are fearful, disoriented, in shock, and no doubt experiencing flashbacks of their leader's traumatic death. In the day we now remember as Holy Saturday, the residue of traumatic death survives.[20] Hope as it had been known died in Jesus. Purpose and meaning died in Jesus. God died in Jesus. The future is incomprehensible. Life itself seems incomprehensible. In the Gospels, except for one small note,[21] this day between is met with silence—the silence of God, the silence of the disciples. Nothing of what had been imagined is possible; only the impossible remains, held in the in-between after the radical ending of something good and an impossible beginning. In this middle space stands the survivor. In this middle space stand the ones who bear witness to the ending and wait before impossibility.

While it is tempting for Christians to jump quickly from the excruciating death of Good Friday to the excitement of resurrection on Easter Sunday,

16. Rambo, *Spirit and Trauma*, 4.

17. Jacques Derrida, quoted in ibid., 25.

18. Ibid., 166.

19. Ibid., 163. Rambo and I both have delved into Jonathan Lear's book to explore hope in the face of sudden traumatic endings. Rambo does some nice work building on Lear's work and the impossibility of hope in survival. See Jonathan Lear, *Radical Hope: Ethics in the Face of Cultural Devastation* (Cambridge, MA: Harvard University Press, 2006). See also Pamela R. McCarroll, "Hopelessness as the Beginning of Hope," unpublished manuscript, given as the Chris Vais Memorial Lecture, Knox College, November 2009.

20. For an elegant and thoughtful exploration of Holy Saturday, see Alan E. Lewis, *Between Cross and Resurrection: A Theology of Holy Saturday* (Grand Rapids: Eerdmans, 2001).

21. Luke 23:56b notes briefly that "On the Sabbath they [the followers of Jesus] rested according to the commandment."

the silent in-betweenness of Holy Saturday and the in-betweenness of life for those who survive traumatic endings challenge us to consider this in-between day as the site where hope as survival comes into fuller view. This is a day when survival is stripped down to the present and the very minute elements of breath, heartbeat, presence, and being. Purpose, meaning, and tomorrow are inconceivable as yet. The very fact of existing points to both the impossibility of what has ended and the impossibility of what yet may be. While it is difficult as postresurrection people to allow this day to open within us in its fullness, the experience of surviving trauma takes us there, whether we like it or not.

The story of Jesus intimates that in the silent void that survives past trauma, we are not alone or isolated in the experience. We are met and accompanied by one who, tradition says, entered fully that day into the inarticulate depths of Sheol, of hell, the place of shadows. Further, the story suggests that even the void, empty silence of post-traumatic survival is held in God. Death, torture, violence, destruction, and the aftermath of survival are all held mysteriously within the whole of the Divine being, within the very womb of God, as Serene Jones describes it.[22] We can sense hope's presence in the historical and spiritual knowledge that Jesus has known such desolation and is present in it. Hope's horizon of participation opens up, even if only in hindsight, when we discover ourselves accompanied to the depths and held within a much larger whole of God's being. Indeed, resurrection confirms the sacred mystery of Holy Saturday, where hope's presence is hidden in the aftermath of trauma, even in death.

We sense hope's presence also in the sheer reality of surviving, still existing in body and breath, as wounded and broken as this may be. Even when no possibility can yet be fathomed, the physical manifestation of impossible possibility remains in *just* surviving. Drawing from Gen. 2:7, the Judeo-Christian tradition holds forth that breath is the essence of the divine presence in life, for it is by God's breath of life that the human became a living being. In the breath of survival, the divine possibility in life remains.[23] Breath itself reflects our participation in relationship with the divine breath of life. Breath embodies both the sign and promise of God's possibility in life. Hope as survival in light of Holy Saturday suggests a kind of waiting—a waiting that is endured in the company of Jesus, is held within the wholeness of God, and through breath

---

22. Serene Jones, "Hope Deferred: Theological Reflections on Reproductive Loss," in *Trauma and Grace: Theology in a Ruptured World* (Louisville: Westminster John Knox, 2009), 127–50.

23. In reflecting on his experience in Auschwitz, Frankl says, "Whoever was still alive had reason for hope." Frankl, *Man's Search for Meaning*, 103. Surviving and hope are inextricably linked here.

and being signifies the presence and promise of transcendent possibility when nothing is conceivable.

CONCLUSION

In post-traumatic situations when people have survived past death and carry the marks of death in life, what does hope-enabling care look like? Clearly, from our discussion so far, we can see that practices of care in such contexts require intentionality in the creation of safe space. Indeed, the provision of safe space is always an important aspect of care. However, in this case, even more attention must be given to the physical, emotional, spiritual, and relational requirements necessary. Further, the survivor him- or herself will be encouraged to develop grounding techniques to help enable his or her own safety. Following trauma recovery theory, care practices will include opportunities for education and the expression of the trauma in ways that honor and respect (and in no way manipulate) the survivor. As well, the expression of trauma will be heard and borne witness to by others who are safe. Care includes opportunities for identifying and mourning what has been lost, perhaps through ritualized means of expression. It also includes opportunities for reconnecting with life and, if possible, actions of advocacy and justice building that address the wrong experienced in the trauma. Central to this process is the affirmation of the person as primary agent, the one to act and to choose—a way of reclaiming the self over against the traumatic experience of having been helpless and overwhelmed. At the same time, hope as survival is not just about agential expressing and enacting. It is also manifested in the sheer experience of having survived, of having breath and life at all. Practices of care here can be manifested in bearing witness to the life that remains and holding hope on behalf of the other. Being present, just present, with people through these times reflects a ministry of presence wherein an incarnational theology of solidarity and accompaniment is represented in the flesh. In being present and holding hope for another, one trusts that the gift of breath present in "just surviving" points beyond itself to divine possibility. One trusts that even there, in the pit of Sheol, the Spirit is present, drawing close in love.

Our exploration of hope as survival has highlighted experiences of hope as these are lived through the trauma recovery process in lives of survivors. This discussion has highlighted the paradoxical character of hope as survival that includes both death and life coexisting in what survives. Through our discussion and the story of Hagar, we have considered ways that the experience of survival itself embodies and points to God's possibility in human life. As well, through discussion of the traumatic death of Jesus and its aftermath, we have sought to carve out a sacred space for hope as survival at the site of Holy Saturday. Indeed, while we may be a postresurrection people, the reality of trauma and its aftermath shatters all certainty and can throw us into Holy Saturday, where any sense of future, meaning, or possibility is nonsensical. Even here, hope as survival remains, opening up horizons of participation amid the inarticulate, fragmented silence of presence, breath, and being.

6

Hope as Lament

My God, my God,
why have you forsaken me?
Why are you so far from helping me,
from the words of my groaning?
O my God, I cry by day, but you do not answer;
and by night, but find no rest.
Ps. 22:1–2

When it was noon, darkness came over the whole land until three in the
afternoon. At three o'clock Jesus cried out in a loud voice, "Eloi, Eloi, lema
sabachthani?" which means, "My God, my God, why have you forsaken
me?"
Mark 15:33–34

The trauma pager calls the chaplain to the emergency room (ER).[1] A teenage boy is being brought in by ambulance. When he was found, after having been stabbed, his condition was vital signs absent (VSA). It does not look good. The victim is taken immediately to the trauma operating room. He is worked on for several minutes until all hope is lost. The bleeding has been too severe. His heart has stopped and cannot be revitalized.

---

1. The case presented in this chapter is a compilation of several experiences in the emergency room. It draws from case notes I have written and discussions I have held with several different families and practitioners in my capacity as an on-call chaplain, supervisor of on-call chaplains, and minister-in-association in a congregation. All names have been changed and details have been added to ensure confidentiality. Other CPE supervisors have reviewed the case and provided input on it.

Within minutes, the panicked parents of the victim come running into the ER, asking for their son. They are directed to the chaplain, who goes with them to the private family waiting room. The attending physician joins them. The chaplain and physician sit near the parents, facing them. The dialogue, written in verbatim format, uses the following abbreviations:[2]

P	Physician
F	Father
M	Mother
C	Chaplain

P1: Hello, I am Dr. B. I am the attending physician for the ER today. I believe you have met our chaplain. *[Parents nod.]* You are the parents of Jethro Hill?

F1: Yes, I am his father, and this is his mother. *[They shake hands.]*

P2: I understand your son was downtown today. *[Parents nod. Pause. Physician sighs.]* I am very sorry to say that when he was brought in here today, he had suffered several stab wounds. We tried for a long time to revive him, but we were unable to do so. *[Stunned silence.]*

F2: What do you mean?

P3: *[Speaking slowly, leaning forward toward parents.]* It seems that he was attacked from behind. . . . Several of his main organs were injured . . . . We tried as best we could . . . . We just couldn't get the bleeding stopped in time. We are very sorry that we couldn't save him.

---

2. This case study is written as a *verbatim report*, a tool for learning commonly used in clinical pastoral education programs and in pastoral care and counseling courses. Everything spoken is identified by a letter in terms of the person speaking (P indicates Physician, F indicates Father, M indicates Mother and so on) and numbered sequentially, increasing in number each time a person speaks. For example, "P1" and "P2" refer to the first and second time the Physician speaks. This formatting enables easy identification of a given statement for the reflective process that follows the verbatim recording of a visit. I chose the verbatim format because it draws from previous written verbatim reports and it allows for greater immediacy and more accurate representation of this case. As well, it provides greater immediacy to the representation of lament in human life.

[Mother gasps, covers her mouth with her hands, and begins to rock, murmuring, "No, no, no . . . ." Father pauses and looks down.]

F3: We want to see him. Can we see him?

C1: *[Speaking slowly with Physician nodding throughout.]* Because it was sudden, the coroner will have to examine him before you can see him.

P4: The police are here, too. They'll need to speak with you. *[Nodding to the chaplain.]* And afterwards the chaplain can take you in to see your son when he is ready. I will be around if you have more questions, OK?

[Parents nod, trying to absorb what they have heard. Physician leaves the room. Mother is rocking and crying. Father is looking down, staring.]

C2: *[Speaking slowly and gently.]* Is there anyone you would like to call to be with you? Other kids, relatives, or someone from your religious community?

M1: *[Speaking through tears.]* Our two youngest are at camp. No need to call them now.

F4: *[Turns head upward suddenly as if getting an idea.]* But we should call Ronnie, our elder at church.

[The parents spend some time trying to remember, and then they find Ronnie's phone number. Father calls on his cell phone. Throughout the call, he is standing and pacing.]

F5: Hi, Ronnie, it's me. . . . Something awful has happened. . . . It's Jethro. . . . He was, I don't know, in a fight, I guess. . . . No, I know he's never been in a fight . . . but, but . . . he was stabbed. . . . I don't know by who. . . . He was stabbed. . . . He's here at the hospital. . . . No *[voice breaking]* . . . no . . . he didn't . . . he didn't make it. . . . *[Breaking down, sobbing.]* . . . No. . . . Mother's here. . . . We haven't seen him. *[Crying.]* . . . Can you come? We're in the ER. . . . OK. . . . OK. . . . The chaplain is here, too. *[Hangs up the phone. Chaplain passes tissues to parents.]*

[Father sits down again by Mother, who is slumped over in her chair, sobbing.]

F6: *[With a surge of anger and confusion raising his voice.]* Who would do this to our boy?! . . . He is a good boy. . . . He isn't involved with bad stuff. . . . We know all his friends. . . . How could this have happened?!

M2: *[Lifts her head.]* We should have been there. One of us should have driven him. He wanted us to, but we were so set on him being more independent. . . . Oh, God! Why didn't we take him?! Why were we so set against it?! I could have gone. I could have taken him! Oh, God . . . .

[Mother leans her head on Father's chest. Both are weeping.]

F7: *[Through tears, sounding desperate.]* But we did what we thought was right. We couldn't have known. We couldn't have known.

C3: No, you couldn't have known. You were trying to do what was best for him.

M3: *[Turning to chaplain, speaking through tears.]* He was so excited about going down to the mall today. He was picking up a new game for the PS3. He and his friend Matt were going to play all night tonight to celebrate the end of school. . . . They were excited. You know how fifteen-year-olds are. . . . *[Pause, absorbing.]* What about Matt? . . . *[Pause, thinking.]* . . . Someone should call Matt. Oh, God, Matt. What's he going to do? *[Intensity escalating.]*

F8: I'll call Ronnie. He can go to the house. He can talk to Matt. *[Calls Elder Ronnie.]* Ronnie . . . no . . . no . . . . We're waiting still. We just think it would be better for you to go to the house. Matt is coming over to meet up with Jethro . . . they were supposed to meet. . . . *[Pause, voice breaking.]* . . . They were supposed to meet to play video games tonight. He has no idea. . . . It will be hard. . . . They've been friends at school and church since they were two years old. . . . You stay with him. . . . *[Voice breaking, crying.]* . . . The chaplain is here, yes. . . . OK, OK.

M 4: Ohhh, God, I just can't believe it. . . . *[Wiping her eyes.]* . . . You hear about this kind of thing on the news but never think it's going to happen to you. . . . What happened? Has anyone given any more information?

C3: The police will meet with you sometime before you leave and may be able to answer some of your questions. I'll go and check on how things are going.

[Chaplain leaves. Returns with drinks.]

C4: They are still examining him. It will be a bit longer, and then you can go in. *[Passing drinks to parents.]* The police can meet with you now. Is that OK? *[Parents nod.]* OK. It's important for you to know that they are trying to piece together what happened, too. Don't worry if you cannot answer some of their questions now. You will have other opportunities to talk with them. I cannot be here when they interview you, but I will wait for you to finish with them, and there is a volunteer from victim services who is here to support you through the interview and after.

M5: Thank you. Thank you. Pray for us.

[Chaplain nods, calls police officer and victim services volunteer, introduces everyone to each other, and leaves. After thirty minutes or so, the chaplain is called back into the room. Police officer and victim services volunteer leave. It is clear that both parents have been crying more throughout the interview and have now settled a bit.]

C5: How did that go?

F9: They said that some of the witnesses have already been interviewed, and they are still piecing things together. . . . But right now it looks like a fight broke out at the exit of the store because our son got one of the last games and another boy was mad that he didn't get one.

M5: The other boy pulled out a knife, and when Jethro refused to give it to him and turned to leave, . . . the boy came after him. . . . Oh, God. . . . *[Weeping, emotional intensity escalating.]*

C6: *[Touches Mother's arm.]* Oh, I'm so sorry, M. . . . *[Mother turns and collapses her head onto the chaplain's shoulder. The chaplain holds her and listens as Father goes on.]*

F10: . . . The other boy came and stabbed him from behind . . . four times. . . . It was deep. . . . He took off with the game. . . . They said there were a lot of witnesses. They don't have the other boy yet, but they expect to find him. . . . A lot of people saw him. . . .

C7: [*Holding Mother and facing Father.*] I know it's terrible for you hearing all this, but it is better for you to get some of the information and begin to piece together a bit of what happened. . . . What an absolute tragedy. . . .

M6: [*Lifting herself, grasping a hand of both Father and the chaplain, putting her head down, sobbing.*] My boy . . . what kind of pain and fear did he feel? Was he just being stubborn? All for a video game. . . . Oh, God . . . it's too much. How could this have happened? . . . I just don't know what to do. [*Breath shortening, perspiring, becoming panicky.*]

C8: [*Holding Mother's hand with both of hers and turning to face her, speaking slowly and clearly.*] Right now, you are where you need to be, M. It's important for you to be here, and we will go in and see him when it is time. . . . Right now, I want you to look at me and take some slow, deep breaths. Breathe in slowly. . . . [*Slowly counting.*] . . . 1-2-3-4-5 . . . . OK, now breathe out slowly, counting to five. . . . 1-2-3-4-5.. . . Good. . . . Now try it again. . . . [*Father and chaplain join in.*]

[*The parents settle somewhat and begin to talk more about their son. They tell the chaplain about his big, warm heart and what a good big brother he was for their younger two kids. They break down at the thought of talking to their other children. They tell about how he made people laugh, especially his grandma, who had a special place in her heart for Jethro, her eldest grandchild. They cry when they talk about how they will tell Grandma about his death. Throughout the conversation, they move between remembering Jethro in the past with joy and then abruptly remembering that he has died, violently. Eventually word comes that they can see their son. After the chaplain checks on Jethro to see what condition he is in and what, if anything, she can do to prepare his body further, she brings the parents into the room.*

They enter the room and see him lying there. Someone takes a deep, audible breath. They pause, and then M runs over and collapses on her son's chest.]

M7: [*Sobbing and crying out.*] Jethro, my Jethro! [*Holding his chest and shaking him.*] No. No. NO! [*Mother collapses, face down into his chest. Chaplain places her hand on Mother's back*]

F11: *[Staring at his son, then falling to his knees.]* How could this happen?! He's a good boy! How?! Oh, God, how could it happen? *[Stays down for a while, then slowly pulls himself back up. He touches his son's face, his cheeks.]* . . . Jethro . . . . Jethro . . . . *[Sobbing, kissing son's cheeks.]*

M8: *[Lifts her head from his chest and looks at him more closely. She begins holding his hand and touching each finger, one at a time.]* Why? Why? Oh, God . . . Oh, God . . . such a precious boy. How could he be taken from us so soon? Why? . . . *[Sobbing continues.]*

F12: *[Settling. Touching Jethro's ear, gently.]* . . . The cut from that terrible fall he had. It's almost starting scarring. . . . *[Caressing his hair.]* Oh, my boy, my boy . . . .

M9: *[Lifting his hand. Kissing it.]* I love these hands. . . . *[Weeping. Holding Jethro's hand to her face . . . pause . . . angrier tone.]* Oh, God, why has this happened to us?

[Weeping and looking, taking in as much as they can.]

C9: Is there anything you would like to say to Jethro?

F13: *[Pausing to consider, then slowly, gently speaking, caressing his face.]* Oh, Jethro, you are a good boy. We love you. We will always love you.

M10: We will always love you. . . . All your life, you've been teaching us how to be parents. . . . You did a good job. I always told you that, . . . but this time . . . oh, God . . . . We should have saved you from this. . . . Why weren't we there? *[Voice breaking, weeping.]* . . . Why didn't God protect him? *[Thrusting her fists onto the side of the stretcher.]*

F14: M, *[Putting his hand on her back looking at Jethro.]* . . . you know what Jethro would say, seeing you like this? . . . He would say what he always likes to say to you: . . . "Don't worry about that, Ma." *[Pause. Remembering. Both weep with a knowing grin.]* We love you, Son. . . . Not a day will go by that we won't be thinking of you.

M11: *[Weeping.]* Yes . . . yes.

[Weeping as they caress his hair, face, and hands.]

C10: Would you like to pray together?
[Parents both nod. As suggested by the chaplain, each parent places a hand on Jethro's head, and they hold each other's hands. The chaplain places a hand on each parent's shoulders.]

Let us pray.
O God, we come to you right now, bodies and souls crying out in anguish,
crying out for help, crying out for comfort, crying out for answers.
We are angry, O God.
We are angry at life, at death, at you, at the person who did this.
How could it happen, O God?
We come to you amid the anger, sadness, and confusion of this time.
[Weeping, Mother and Father add, "Yes, Lord . . . yes, Lord."]
We come to you with all sorts of things surging through us.
We don't understand, but we seek some comfort—
comfort that only you can give, even while we rage and weep.
[Weeping, "Yes, Lord. Yes, Lord."]
We thank you for Jethro, the precious son of M and F.
[Weeping, "Yes. Yes."]
Thank you for all the ways he has made life rich and precious.
Thank you that he has loved and been loved so fiercely.
[Weeping, "Yes, Lord. Yes, Lord."]
Help us, O God. Help M and F entrust their precious Jethro to you, O God.
As difficult as it is, help them release him to your care, assured that he is safe and whole with you. Comfort them, O God. Comfort them . . . . [Pause.]
We pray in Jesus name, Amen. ["Amen, Amen."]

[After some final kisses, the three leave the room. With the chaplain they arrange for next steps and follow up, and after a final embrace M and F leave for home.]

REFLECTING WITH JETHRO'S PARENTS

How do we begin to explore the possibility of hope being present amid the anguished lament of parents grieving the death of their son by senseless violence? How can we possibly imagine hope being present at such a time without distorting the harshness and making it something that it is not? How do we speak of hope here without doing violence to people who have already lost so much? Is the attempt to discern hope here merely an attempt to "pretty up" and avoid the terrible agony that overwhelms such moments of extreme loss? These questions point to important cautions for us as we dare tread on fragile terrain—looking to discern hope's presence even where all is lost. The hope we are seeking here is not one that is full of brightness and light. Rather, it is a hope that is hidden within the anguish of parents' lament, a hope that is embedded within their anger and their embrace, their crying out and their tender touch.

In the parents' outburst of grief and their bodies' shock responses, the depth and breadth of their love for their dead son is fully exposed. Within the gasps and tears of mourning, we hear lives torn open by the loss of one well loved, one who is precious and irreplaceable. This love is embodied. It is full-bodied. It lives in the interconnected fabric of this family, and now, with the death of a beloved son, the fabric of interconnectedness is torn open. It is as if a part of their body has been ripped out. The pain is overwhelming. The parents' cries of anguish and lament reflect the backside of life lived and life loved—the backside of thanksgiving and gratitude for a son's life. Within their cries is a love that knows no bounds. In their lament, the gifts of life and love are carried with the full burden of their truth. Hope murmurs in the expression of ruptured love.

In crying out their pain, these parents give voice and expression to what's wrong. It is a cry of protest against what has happened. They cannot be silenced by the weight of unfairness or even a sense of guilt or responsibility, which, though present, is subsumed by their cries of "How? Why?" In wailing against the violent death of their son, they join the refrain of all who protest against suffering and persecution. They join the voices of those who live the burdens of unfairness in life, saying, "All is not right with the world, and we cannot abide it. All is not right with the world, and it should not be so."

In some sense also, in expressing the chaos and the tearing apart of their lives as they have known them, their words and bodies point beyond the chaos itself and give voice to that which makes no sense, to a rupturing too deep for words. The chaos is heard and given some shape and space to be represented. Indeed, these words of lament at the deathbed of their son mark only the beginning of a lament that will last a lifetime. But the compulsion to express, to live fully, to protest and speak out the chaotic reality of what is happening also points beyond the unfairness and injustice of the chaos itself. Hope murmurs here where the desperation for something beyond the chaos of the present moment is intimated.

Their mourning cry also points to both the shock and the embrace of finitude. At some level, their cries acknowledge the shock of finitude that includes the devastating fragility of existence in which a much-loved son could be killed on a beautiful, sunny day. At another level, their cries reflect a full giving over of themselves to their own finitude, frailty, and inability to change what has happened. In their laments, they reflect the sheer limit of being human in the face of death. It is in the embracing of their finitude that their cries ring up to heaven for a comfort and a peace that is beyond their capacity to generate.

Throughout the interaction (F6, F11; M6, M8, M9, M10, C10), the anger, sorrow and confusion of Jethro's parents is placed before God. Their direct cries out to God (F11, M8, M9, M10) suggest an ongoing and hearty relationship with a God they trust enough to give themselves over to with a sense of abandon. They are free to be confused before God, feel angry at God, and call out for comfort to God all at once. Their faith suggests a freedom *to be* that is reminiscent of the Hebrew Psalmists. They do not pretend to have any sense of mastery over circumstance, over God, or even over themselves. The dynamism of their relationship with this God is trusted for what it is without pretense, without any sense of where it will go, without fear. This level of trust even in the face of devastation points to hope's possibility even when it is inconceivable.

What does care look like for Jethro's parents? Over the months and years, care for them will come in the form of shared rituals of remembering and through prayer, both communal and individual. It will come through safe people with whom they can lament and in communal opportunities for mourning. It will come through people who can be present with them in the waves of pain, anger, confusion, and sorrow that will continue to erupt at different moments. Care will come in the ways they are accompanied through the trial process and the ways they are companioned through the challenges to forgive and to be released from rage at the other boy. Care will come in the tiny and big ways that Jethro's life is remembered among those who knew him—including him in memories of the past, talking about him naturally, and participating in shared opportunities to mourn, remember, and give thanks for Jethro and the ways his life and his death have changed people.

How does this experience of lament at the deathbed of their son reflect our definition of hope? Indeed, Jethro's parents experience the shutting down of possibility and the closing of horizons of meaning and participation upon the death of their son. In some sense, hope as it has been known to them in their lives thus far is impossible. However, in a backward way, the depth of their love for Jethro, the sense of their own limit and finitude, their protest against chaos and yearning for purpose all represent the ways hope is present in hidden ways through this encounter.

One way to get at the hope that is embedded in lament is to imagine a sudden and tragic death such as Jethro's existing in the world without care. Imagine that there was no one to lament and protest his passing: no one to weep over him and caress his hands and head, no one to cry out against God and life on his behalf, no one to remember with love the particularities of who he was. What if his life and death were met with indifference, as if his being did not matter? Such indifference defies both hope and hopelessness. In the face of a death such as this, would not such indifference feed into a sense that nothing matters and that chaos and meaninglessness rule supreme? But such is not the case. The tortured honesty of these parents' laments testify fiercely to a life much loved. Where love is present, hope is never far behind. For love reflects the opening of horizons of meaning and participation in relation with otherness even in the others' absence.

Jethro's parents are explicit about their faith and the fact that God is deeply implicated in their lives and in the terrible tragedy that has overtaken them. Their willingness to be angry and to raise questions to God reflects the long-standing character of their relationship with God. More importantly, it reflects the heartiness of their faith in which they trust enough to bring their whole selves, broken, helpless, and angry as they are, before God. They will not hide their jaggedness and anger. Rather, they claim relationship with God in the very midst of their tribulations. Even in their anger, sorrow, and confusion, the fact that they cry out to God represents the opening of horizons, the possibility of hope. When they come to their limit, they cry out for God's help.

The parents' lament resists chaos and meaninglessness as the final word. It seeks a larger whole, a larger horizon of meaning, which is recognized most profoundly by its apparent absence in the moment of lament itself. Their cries embody a desperate yearning for that which is known most fully because of its absence: the longing for relationship with a lost son, with a past life, with God, who can set things right. Hope's possibility persists in this yearning that reaches out beyond the temporal, beyond present circumstance, beyond all that is visible to the naked eye. It is the hidden presence of hope that compels the lament to decry the absence of God, of meaning, of hope. It is the hidden presence of hope that compels the lament to tear open the gates of eternity so that a larger horizon may come into view.

Possibilities and Limits

Grief is love's alter ego ... the necessary other.... How may we know light without knowledge of the dark? How may we know love without sorrow? ... Grief gives the full measure of love, and it is somehow reassuring to learn, even by suffering, how large and powerful love is.
Jane F. Maynard[3]

Mourning and wonder, neither one answers the question that trauma poses to grace. They are, instead, states of mind that, if nurtured open us to experience God's coming into torn flesh, and love's arrival amidst violent ruptures.
Serene Jones[4]

The connection between lament and hope has been an important one throughout the Judeo-Christian traditions and recently has been re-claimed as an area of focus within pastoral theology. In particular there has been an emphasis on the Psalms of lament and complaint as illuminating resources for contemporary people struggling with major loss, grief, disaster and crisis. Central to the contemporary focus on lament is the extent to which such expression is not only therapeutic in its cathartic release and dynamic in its expression of faith but also, through protest and resistance, participates in making a more just world.

Walter Brueggemann has done a great deal of work on the Psalms of lament and complaint so as to open them up as resources for contemporary faith in hard times.[5] Pastoral theologians have drawn extensively on Brueggemann's work. He identifies that nearly half of all the Psalms are songs of lament and complaint: "Something is known to be deeply amiss in Israel's life with God. And Israel is not at all reluctant to voice what is troubling about its life."[6] These Psalms, he argues, reflect a spirituality of protest in which "Israel boldly

---

3. Jane F. Maynard, *Transfiguring Loss: Julian of Norwich as a Guide for Survivors of Traumatic Grief* (Cleveland: Pilgrim, 2006), 13.

4. Serene Jones, *Trauma and Grace: Theology in a Ruptured World* (Louisville: Westminster John Knox, 2009), 161.

5. See, among other books, Brueggemann, *Spirituality of the Psalms* (Minneapolis: Fortress, 2002).

6. Walter Brueggemann, foreword to *Psalms of Lament*, by Ann Weems (Louisville: Westminster John Knox, 1995), xi.

recognizes that all is not right in the world. . . . But Israel also defiantly refuses to confess its guilt or to take responsibility for what's wrong in the world."[7] The Psalms of lament and complaint illustrate a recurring and disciplined form and structure. Israel, Brueggemann says, "knew how to order its grief, not only to get that grief fully uttered and delivered but also to be sure that, said in its fullness untameable, it is not turned loose with destructiveness."[8] Brueggemann does much to demonstrate the extent to which the Psalms of lament and complaint are structured and ordered with a recognizable pattern.[9] The structure enables the rawness of lament to be directed in particular and faithful ways. These Psalms challenge contemporary people of faith to participate, as part of the practice of faith, in crying out against what is wrong in the world. They urge us to be honest and real before God and with each other amid temptations otherwise, and they push us to greater trust, that we might enter the depths of pain and there be opened to unexpected grace.

Brueggemann's work on the Psalms stands in agreement with modern psychological theories that emphasize the importance of expressing and giving voice to pain in the process of healing. The utterance of lament is cathartic, releasing us from the stranglehold of pain: "Everything must be brought to speech and everything brought to speech must be addressed to God who is the final reference for all of life."[10] The Psalms of lament reflect faith in God, who is "attentive to the darkness, weakness, and displacement of life."[11] Brueggemannn contends that Psalms of lament and complaint are also performative in the sense that such speech itself "works a new reality," calling on God for intervention, transformation, and miracle. The utterance of lament itself participates in the coming of new possibility, which, without it, is impossible.[12] The Psalms of lament invite hope because they point to a reality outside of the immediate, beyond "the pitiful regimes [and ways] of the present age [that] claim to be

---

7. Ibid., xii.

8. Ibid., xi.

9. Ibid., xi. The pattern begins with the "naming of God in an intimate address." Second, it moves to complaint, stating the extremity of pain, to get God's attention. Third is the petition for God to turn, heed, save. Fourth, the complaint moves into regressive speech, with motivations for God to act added to the petition. Often the dialogue will then turn to vengeance against an enemy who has caused the hurt. And finally, "when the need, the hurt, the demand, and the venom are fully voiced, something unexpected happens in the psalm." The psalm turns to praise and rejoicing for God's bountiful grace and mercy.

10. Brueggemann, *Spirituality of the Psalms*, 27.

11. Ibid., 27.

12. Brueggemann, foreword to *Psalms of Lament*, xiii.

and seem [to be] absolute and eternal." Through lament, we bear witness to the ultimately provisional character of all present power arrangements.[13]

In his foreword to Ann Weems's *Psalms of Lament*, in which she shares poems she has written in the aftermath of the violent death of her son Todd, Brueggemann states, "The life of the poet, like the life of the world is saturated with pain and ache not yet finished, not yet answered, not yet resolved. And we are left with the demanding question, What shall we do with so much of hurt that is left unfinished?"[14] The response to this question comes in the form of Psalms of lament. Just as Weems does in lamenting the death of her beloved son, we are challenged by the Psalms to speak, cry, and rage our sorrow, our confusion, our anger in the face of life's harshness. As Weems says, "There is no salvation in self help books; the help we need is far beyond self. Our only hope is to march ourselves to the throne of God and in loud lament cry out the pain that lives in our souls."[15] While Weems expresses that her psalms of lament in this world will be forever incomplete, she does note that shifts have occurred within her. Lament has opened up also to alleluias: "Anger and alleluias careen around within me, sometimes colliding. Lamenting and laugher sit side by side in a heart that yearns for peace that passes understanding."[16]

Drawing on Brueggemann's work, Swinton explores the importance of "lament for resisting evil and dealing faithfully with suffering."[17] Lament, he argues, "provides us with language of outrage that speaks against the way things are, but always in the hope . . . [of] change."[18] It provides those who suffer "with hopeful language in which they can wrestle with God, self, others as they attempt to make sense."[19] Sometimes, he contends, lament is the only language of hope available.[20] It is the language of faithfulness in the face of the harshness and suffering of life.

Both Jean Stairs and Serene Jones, drawing similarly on work with the Psalms, contend that the movement into the chaos and cry of lament is essential for the spiritual journey to hope in the face of loss and crisis. People must be encouraged to "enter the time of chaos, contradiction and liminality more

13. Brueggemann, *Spirituality of the Psalms*, 55.

14. Brueggemann, foreword to *Psalms of Lament*, ix.

15. Weems, *Psalms of Lament*, xvi.

16. Ibid., xvi.

17. John Swinton, *Raging with Compassion: Pastoral Responses to the Problem of Evil* (Grand Rapids: William B. Eerdmans, 2007), 5.

18. Ibid., 104–105.

19. Ibid., 129.

20. Ibid., 222.

deeply, and naming and lamenting what is dying or whatever needs to die. There is a chaos that is part of the dying process. . . . If there is rage at God it must be heard into speech."[21] Lament comes upon us in moments of raw grief, but it is also a cathartic, communal act, "expressing the unfinished ache of death" in this realm.[22] In making a link between lament and hope, Stairs argues that lament begins at the tomb and ends at the soul's awakening to the limits of hope and resurrection:[23] "Even when God seems . . . absent, it is in voicing despair that the soul is most keenly alive to the reality of God. The power of hope is enacted in the utterance of despair. New life comes through an embrace of death whenever we find it implanted into our lives. . . . The pastoral work of lament is this simultaneous resistance and embrace of every pressure toward new life."[24] We can see the extent to which the Psalms of lament and complaint have become an important resource for contemporary pastoral theologians to think through the interconnectedness of practices of lament and the possibility of hope in the face of adversity and trauma.

One of the primary reasons I believe that the theology and practice of lament has recently become an important focus is the fact that in our fast-paced, impatient, and technologically driven context, little space is given for the expression of lament. As a society, we have neglected communal practices of lament, yet in the face of devastating tragedies of the past decade or so, we have found ourselves desperate for opportunities to mourn and lament together. As the church has increasingly moved to the periphery of North American (especially Canadian) society, the structured forms of lament that used to ritualize and channel public mourning are no longer shared. At the same time, however, over the last several years, spontaneous communal expressions of lament have begun to emerge in the face of public tragedies, death, and violence. Consider, for example, the death of any number of famous (or infamous) people and the memorial artifacts left by members of the public at specific sites.[25] We now commonly see shrines of lament at sites where death

21. Jean Stairs, *Listening for the Soul: Pastoral Care and Spiritual Direction* (Minneapolis: Fortress Press, 2004), 90–91. Similarly, Jones says that in lament, we "learn to enter pain as if it were the arms of God. . . . Trust is the first ally of hope." David Lee Jones, "A Pastoral Model for Caring for Persons with Diminished Hope." *Pastoral Psychology* 58 (2009), 660.

22. Ibid., 94.

23. Ibid., 94–95.

24. Ibid., 97.

25. In my area of the world, a series of highways have been named the "Highway of Heroes" to honor the many dead Canadian soldiers whose bodies arrived from Afghanistan to the military airport at Trenton, Ontario, and then were driven to the coroner's office in downtown Toronto. While the practice of honouring soldiers who had died began quietly, as the public became aware that the bodies of

or trauma has transpired—along highways, on street corners, in school yards and parks, and outside homes and recreation centers. Such gestures suggest that there is an elemental human need for shared actions and spaces of lament as a way to give voice to, among other things, both the meaningfulness of life and the shock of death. In the church and the public sphere, the more we make space for shared enactments of lament in the face of violence, death, and destruction, the more we honor the gift that life is and commit to its nurturance.

One area of caution that emerges in considering our theme is concern that people can get caught in lament without ceasing. Rethinking lament as hope may only encourage people to be caught in the experience of lament. There are two ways to consider this concern. First, the pattern of lament evidenced in the Psalms and in life suggests that while it may be repeated over a lifetime, the enacting of lament itself leads to release and to the possibility for grace to be experienced. Stairs and others suggest that if one seems caught in lament, it may mean that one has not entered fully enough into the depth of pain itself as a shared communal act. It is when one entrusts oneself to experience the fullness of the agony and pain of lament, particularly in community, that release transpires and grace emerges. Divine presence finds us there. Second, the form and structuring of the Psalms of lament and complaint suggest that such energies must be directed and given shape. As Brueggemann argues, the Hebrew people were aware that mourning and lament can be turned to destructive ends that undermine, rather than build up the sense of interconnectedness and relationship with life and creation. The chaotic energies that emerge following devastation on a personal or collective level can fuel a destructive revenge or self harm. Indeed, even most of the Psalms of lament include vengeful thoughts toward the enemy. But these words of vengeance, these destructive energies, are placed before God, rather than acted upon. For those caught in cycles of lament in which destructive energies predominate, it may be important to explore how these energies might be better directed—laid before God or in actions that externalize and concretize the experience of lament itself.

This raises the question regarding the possibility to lament for those who are not people of faith. Indeed, when no transcendent Other is presumed to hear the cries of lament, what becomes of such cries? Where can hope as lament

---

soldiers were being transported along this corridor, the journey from the airport to the coroner's office became a procession, complete with a police escort and highway signposts. Massive numbers of people would line bridges and wait for the procession to pass by. In silence, they would gather to wait, remember, mourn, and honor these slain young men and women. Waiting along the Highway of Heroes became a shared enactment of lament and mourning.

emerge if there is no Other to whom our cries are directed? What makes hope as lament "effective"? Is it all contingent upon directing our lament to some Divine Other? Let's explore these questions from a few different angles. First, the use of the Psalms as a resource for contemporary pastoral theological discussions of lament generally presupposes faith in a Divine Other and lament as an expression of mourning that generally is addressed to this Divine Other. While the character of lament is shaped by framing it as an address to God and while the possibilities for hope as lament are deeply formed by the faith relationship that is presupposed therein, my understanding of lament does not limit it to the intentional addressing of God by people of faith. I include in lament all expressions of mourning and crying out of the "Why?" and "How?" questions in the face of devastating loss. Scripture and tradition affirm that God is creator of all things, including those within and outside of covenants of faith. The life and witness of Jesus reveals a God responsive to the cries and yearnings of those within and outside the covenant of faith.[26] By faith we can confess that God hears the laments that surge forth from both those who claim and those do not claim faith, those who address God directly and those who imagine no transcendent other to hear and receive their cries. In some sense the efficacy of lament exists in the lament itself.

Second, the importance of lament being heard and even shared by other people is central to the possibility for hope as lament. While human others do not replace the Divine Other as hearer, in some sense their presence represents the Divine Other, bears witness to the loss, and embodies a larger whole within which the lament is held. As one called to care for those inside and outside specific faith traditions, I have often drawn on the image of Job's friends who come to him in his distress, who sit with him, weep with him, and wait with him:

> Now when Job's three friends heard of all these troubles that had come upon him, each of them set out from his home . . . . They met together to go and console and comfort him. When they saw him from a distance, they did not recognize him, and they raised their voices and wept aloud; they tore their robes and threw dust in the air upon their heads. They sat with him on the ground seven days and seven nights, and no one spoke a word to him, for they saw that his suffering was very great. (Job 2:11-13)

26. See, for example, the story of the Syrophoenician woman and Jesus' responsiveness to her in Mark 7:24-30; Matt. 15:21-28.

For me, the actions of these friends embody the ministry of presence to which I am called as a chaplain. Such presence in the midst of pain and anguish represents the existential and historical reality that the one at the center of lament is not alone, abandoned, or isolated. It bears witness to the meaningfulness of life and relationship and the pain of its ending. The practice of sitting together and sharing in acts of lament, even when God's presence is not presupposed, opens up horizons of possibility. Grief shared in communal lament bears witness to a larger whole within which life exists and participates and thereby manifests hope's possibility.

Standing at the center of hope as lament in the Christian narrative is Jesus, betrayed, tortured, mocked, hanging on a cross, crying out to God his piercing words, "My God, my God, why have you forsaken me?" (Mark 15:34b) At the height of his agony, Jesus rails out the question that all who suffer cry out: Why? In uttering his words of lament and bringing to expression the experience of God's absence, Jesus enters fully into the alienating power of darkness and death that prey upon the world. Jesus finds himself abandoned, separated from God's presence, unable to be comforted by thoughts of redemption, purpose, or meaning, caught in the very midst of the chaos. Jesus' lament rages at God in desperation but also believes in God as God. That this story is a central story of the Christian Scriptures bears witness to the ways hope is truly present in lament. In entering fully into human suffering, facing the ferocity of the powers of death and destruction, and in crying out to God in the very midst of this, Jesus accompanies all those who suffer and joins in their lament. In the midst of the worst assaults life can throw at us, the story of Jesus' death on the cross reminds us that Jesus meets us there, accompanies us there, represents us there, and invites us to follow him in crying out, even and especially when we experience the shock of divine absence. May Jesus' lament embolden our own, calling on God in those moments when all seems lost, that we may, in our cries, participate in the opening of the horizon of hope.

CONCLUSION

In times of overwhelming loss and shock, when all that is known is a crying out against what is, what does hope-enabling care look like? Indeed, as we have seen in such situations, care practices include space carved out for the sounds and fury of lament. As waves of grief crash in upon those who have lost so much, care includes encouragement to release the intensity and furor that swirls within and a compassionate presence that perseveres alongside, bearing witness to lament and the love it represents. Most importantly, it means letting lament be lament. It means trusting the process and not jumping in to pretty things up. Sometimes care in these instances may include helping people release their anger at God and making links with the biblical companions in the faith, the psalmists and others, whose faith had the vibrancy to entrust even their rage and anger to God. At the same time, care in such contexts includes creating opportunities for the release of lament that is constructive and can point toward healing possibility. One obvious example of this practice is the funeral or memorial service where the community is gathered together to collectively mourn and raise up in thanksgiving the precious particularity of what has been lost, what is mourned. In participating in collective lament, those who have lost so much experience themselves to be surrounded and enfolded such that their lament is joined with that of many others, including those standing at the foot of the cross. They know themselves to be grounded in a larger web of relationality that holds them and accompanies them in their sorrow. This kind of communal enactment represents, embodies, and points to the transcendent solidarity of God-with-us. Further, regular opportunities on special days and high holidays to join in collective lament, remembering, and thanksgiving can open horizons of meaning and participation in relation to life and life's possibility in time.

In this chapter, we have explored the ways the practice of lament embodies hope by opening up horizons of meaning and participation that have otherwise been closed. While hope as lament includes within it a deeply paradoxical reality, it points to the ways that even the most devastating of experiences cannot separate us from hope's presence, even as it remains mostly hidden. We have considered hope as lament in terms of its cathartic therapeutic intent, in terms of its expression of protest against chaos and its yearning for a meaning that transcends the chaos. We have considered it as an expression of deep faith and trust in a Divine Other who hears and responds. We have considered the importance of communal hearing and sharing in lament as an important element of hope's horizon opening up. Finally, we have considered the extent to which Christians believe that those who lament are met by Christ, who not only bears witness to the truth of their lament but also points to the impossible possibility of new life, even when all is lost.

I will close this chapter by sharing one of the poems of lament written by Ann Weems that points to belief and the presence of Christ in the very midst of deep mourning and grief:

In quiet times this image comes to me: Jesus weeping.
Jesus wept,
And in his weeping,
He joined himself forever
To those who mourn.
He stands now throughout all time,
This Jesus weeping,
With his arms about the weeping ones:
"blessed are those who mourn,
for they will be comforted."
He stands with the mourners,
For his name is God-with-us.
Jesus wept.[27]

27. Weems, *Psalms of Lament*, xvi. Used with permission of Westminster John Knox Press.

7

Hope as Surrender

He came out and went, as was his custom, to the Mount of Olives; and the
disciples followed him. . . . Then he withdrew from them about a stone's
throw, knelt down, and prayed, "Father, if you are willing, remove this cup
from me; yet, not my will but yours be done."
Luke 22:39, 41-42

When they came to the place that is called The Skull, they crucified Jesus .
. . . Then Jesus said, "Father, forgive them; for they do not know what they
are doing."
Luke 23:33a, 34

It was now about noon, and darkness came over the whole land until three
in the afternoon, while the sun's light failed; and the curtain of the temple
was torn in two. Then Jesus, crying with a loud voice, said, "Father, into
your hands I commend my spirit." Having said this, he breathed his last.
Luke 23:44-46

When Chris was diagnosed, he was a vital, healthy, thirty-five-year-old man,
newly married and serving as a minister with the Presbyterian Church in
Canada in Waterdown, Ontario, where he had served for almost ten years.[1] His
story is shared primarily through his own words. [2]

1. Susan McLeod, "A Note," in Vais, *For Words*, 1.
2. The story of Chris Vais is taken and adapted entirely from Chris Vais, *For Words: A Journal of Hope
and Healing* (Guelph, ON: Susan McLeod, 2003). This book includes all the issues of the journal *For
Words*, published during Chris's life when he was living with ALS. I am grateful to the Vais family for

I was diagnosed as having ALS on January 13th, 1997, a Monday. That date divides my life into two parts: before and after. A neurologist had administered some tests on the previous Friday, during which time he asked one of the Top Ten Questions You Don't Want to Hear From Your Doctor.

"Are you aware of any neuromuscular disease in your family history?"

"Uh, no. I don't think so. Why?"

"Well, I want you to examine these results more closely over the weekend. Come to my office on Monday. And you might want to bring your wife."

Gulp. "OK."

. . . Monday finally came and we were sitting in the neurologist's office.

Wasting no time, he said, "The news is not good. I'm fairly certain you have amyotrophic lateral sclerosis, or ALS."

Amyo-what? I thought to myself, while glancing at Susan, who looked as scared and confused as I was.

"It's better known as Lou Gehrig's Disease. We don't know what causes it and there is no known cure. It's a progressive, fatal disease that attacks the motor neurons causing the muscles to weaken. The average survival rate after diagnosis is three to five years, although some people live longer than that."

". . . I am very sorry," he said as we stood up to leave, "If you have any further questions, give me a call."

Susan and I left the building in stunned silence. It was a brilliant mid-winter day. Sunlight sparkled off the banks of snow that rose between the street and the sidewalk. As we walked hand in hand towards the car, I breathed deeply of the crisp, cold air. I noticed a woman a few steps ahead of us pushing a stroller. A balding man in a business suit and unbuttoned trench coat leaned casually against a mailbox and chattered into his cell phone. Three high school students sharing a single cigarette huddled together in front of a

their review of and input on this chapter and to Susan McLeod for her support and for granting permission for extensive quoting of For Words in this chapter.

cafe. The appearance of normalcy was startling. I thought, don't they realize I'm dying? I've just been handed some life-shattering information and the world seems to be carrying on as if nothing was wrong. How can this be? It felt like the plug had been pulled and I was starting to spiral down the drain. We reached the car and got in. As we drove away, the tears flowed freely.[3]

Chris continued to serve in that congregation for about a year and a half after the diagnosis until the illness forced him out of congregational ministry. It was at this difficult time that he discerned a call to continue ministry through *For Words: A Journal of Hope and Healing*. *For Words* was published four times a year, and through it, Chris invited others into his journey—his debilitating struggle with ALS and the wrestling of his faith in the face of ALS—with the intention to feed hope and healing in others experiencing difficult times. With support from his wife, Susan, his family, and friends, he continued making regular journal entries until a couple of weeks before his death in June 2002.

Throughout the journal, Chris describes his experiences of loss—the loss of his ability to play guitar, to sing, to preach, to speak, to walk, to hug, to eat, and more. He shares the pain and sorrow, sadness and anger that accompany these losses and what the loss of specific abilities means for his day-to-day life. He also shares his insights and reflections on suffering and grace, prayer and community by looking at life from the angle of one living with ALS. He shares many experiences of blessing amid the harshness of this disease. As his illness progressed, the work required for Chris to type in the letters for each word of *For Words* became increasingly painstaking, a physical sacrifice and a gift offered at a cost.

In his first entry, titled "Too Deep for Words," Chris describes how he realized his voice was changing while preaching on Pentecost Sunday:

> On that Sunday morning last May I too felt like I was speaking in another tongue. I was bewildered and afraid, overcome by a sinking feeling that I, a preacher, was beginning to lose my voice.
>
> Much later I learned that I was experiencing the early stages of dysarthria, a weakening of the muscle groups involved in speaking, a common problem for people with ALS. . . . [It is] a scary thing to be losing my ability to speak. Given that a fundamental characteristic of human behaviour is the capacity to communicate through language,

3. Vais, *For Words*, 30–31.

and that the essentials of ministry—preaching, administering the sacraments, teaching, pastoral care—depend upon the good use of words, the prospect of being unable to talk has been extremely distressing. I preached my last sermon on September 20, 1998.[4]

The inability to communicate as he had through spoken word got Chris thinking about prayer and the use and meaning of words in our communication with God. He wrote, "Prayer has more to do with listening than talking. It is more about being than doing. It is the experience of coming into the presence of One much greater than oneself. This goes far beyond mere words. It is an experience too deep for words."[5]

During this time, Chris also found himself sighing frequently. The deep, long sighs were attempts to get oxygen to parts of his body that were lacking it. However, he also wondered about the meaning of his sighing: "Maybe my sighing is an expression of the sorrow and sadness I feel, the acute sense of loss that inevitably comes with a disease like ALS."[6] Sighing, even the sighs of sorrow and sadness, became the means to prayer. Chris quotes Rom. 8:26: "The Spirit helps us in our weakness; for we do not know how to pray as we ought, but that very Spirit intercedes with sighs too deep for words."[7] He invites his readers to join with him in his sighing prayer. "This is my prayer: YHWH. Try it with me. YH . . . (breathing in) . . . WH . . . (breathing out). I offer this prayer every time I sigh. It reminds me of the Holy One whose name is [YHWH,] I-WILL-BE-THERE (Exodus 3:13-14)."[8] Inarticulate as a word itself, full of mystery and depth, he invites us to join him in sighing our prayers to "the One who is there in the short sweet breath of a baby newborn, in the long laboured breathing when the end is near, taking us to places too deep for words."[9]

After Chris and Susan had moved in with his parents in Muskoka, Ontario, and within a few days of home care starting for Chris, their daughter, Clare, was born. In an entry titled "God Comes as a Child," Chris writes about his relationship with Clare, often mixed with expressions of fullness of joy and sorrow:

4. Vais, For Words, 3–4.
5. Ibid., 5.
6. Ibid., 6.
7. Ibid., 7.
8. Ibid.
9. Ibid.

One of the saddest things about having this disease right now is that I am unable to hold our daughter Clare. The muscles in my hands and arms have weakened to the extent that I do not have strength to either lift or support her twenty pounds on my own. Nevertheless I touch her and talk to her frequently. Voice and touch are important ways of conveying love and security. So I lean into her crib in the morning and greet her with slurred words and nasal tones. Sometimes I sing to her, despite sounding like a drunk in a midnight choir, I brush my curled fingers against her tummy and legs and gently rub her cheek with the back of my thin atrophied hand. She pushes at me playfully. . . . Although I cannot hold her, she does sit on my lap supported by a nursing pillow. . . . They say children of disabled parents learn at an early age not to wiggle and squirm when sitting together. They learn to hold on while being held. They somehow know instinctively to be still. I am confident that Clare will learn this way of being with me. Meanwhile I wonder if I can learn this way of being with God. I wiggle and squirm under the demands of that Presence. I need to hold on as well as be held. I need to be still. . . . It is as simple and as profound as that. . . . Simple, perhaps, but not easy. Not for me, at least. . . . Surrendering control is not easy. But it's the only way to live by faith.[10]

In this same entry Chris continues to ponder what he will face in his future.

Living with ALS, I have tried to be realistic regarding the implications of the disease. Harbouring few illusions, I am aware of the path it will likely take. At the same time I live in hope, taking one step at a time. I try to dwell in the here and now, not letting my thoughts creep too far towards some imaginary future state. . . . It is a fine balance between despair and hope, between fear and faith. It is a fine balance between letting this disease take my life and entrusting it to God. Worrying about the future is like climbing a tree and crawling out on a limb. The farther I go, the more likely the branch will break and I'll plummet to the ground. When it comes to being anxious about tomorrow, the limb may be imaginary, but the fall is painfully real. It's a dangerous game that results in panic, then

10. Ibid., 26-29.

depression, which in turn wreaks havoc on my entire being. During my darker moments, when I get too far out there, I cling to those words of the Lord recorded by the Psalmist, "Be still, and know that I am God."[11]

Under the title "Dreams of Wholeness," Chris discusses suffering, prayer, and healing at length. He affirms what has become for him an important distinction between healing and cure and he explores ways divine energy heals when illness persists even unto death:

In the midst of [my] having ALS, the Holy Spirit is drawing me closer to God. This experience is deepening my prayer life, teaching me invaluable lessons about the love of God that I never could have learned otherwise. It has laid me open to the generous, sacrificial love of God's people. It has created in me a new compassion for the many people in God's world who suffer dreadfully, and has increased my desire to do something about their pain. Even as I grow weaker, God's Spirit is strengthening my sense of purpose in my life and ministry. Therefore my first prayer is not that I might be cured of ALS (although I am open to that possibility). My first prayer is that, no matter what happens, I may have the strength and courage to be a faithful disciple of Jesus Christ. Out of obedience to Christ, I am called to cooperate with God's highest will for wholeness, health and salvation.[12]

The final entry written by Chris was the first issue of volume 4, titled "Beyond Words." Here Chris shares his many reflections on death, his deep sense of sadness, and possibilities for wholeness and the afterlife:

I think about death a lot. The thought of dying enters my mind nearly every day. I've possessed this mindset since January 13, 1997. . . . On that cold, clear winter's day over five years ago, like a shadowy acquaintance from a faraway land, death came calling. . . .

The wretched ailment has reached so far into me now that its greedy fingers have slowly strangled most of my muscles, including the ones that allow me to breathe. A blood test taken [recently] . . .

11. Ibid., 29.
12. Ibid., 75.

revealed a high level of CO_2 in my system. In other words, because my breathing is weak, I'm not getting enough oxygen in my blood. Also, because my diaphragm and other muscles have deteriorated, I'm not able to expel the used air that contains waste carbon dioxide. Retaining the bad air manifests in many symptoms. . . . I never really feel rested because, whenever I start to doze, I stop breathing. My bobbing head jerks upwards. I sputter and gasp for air, like a drowning man hauled up over the side of a boat. . . .

All this has got me thinking more about death. My death. . . . Of course I don't know exactly when I'm going to die, but I know it won't be long. I want to be as prepared as possible. . . . Neither do I know how. Like most people with ALS, I'll probably die by suffocation. The muscles that allow me to breathe will weaken to the point where I won't be able to draw another breath. While the prospect of this frightens me, I don't feel paralyzed by that fear. I expect to die peacefully and in relative comfort. I have few regrets, no enemies that I know of, no outstanding grudges that require reconciliation, and no significant items that I haven't already ticked off on my life's "to do" list.

I'll be turning 40 this October. Dying at such a young age causes me to feel a deep, aching sadness. I go through times of feeling sorry for myself. I feel sad when I think of Clare, and how I won't be there to celebrate her graduation from high school, or to walk her down the aisle on her wedding day. I won't be there to lend her (or her mother) a hand through those times of rapid change and development from childhood to adolescence to adulthood. It breaks my heart to think of Susan, and to consider all the dreams that this disease has shattered. No more strolls down the beach hand in hand. No more leisurely meals at a favourite restaurant. No more tender whispers in the ear in a candlelit room. The wound deepens with the realization that I've now had ALS for over half the time we've known each other. We won't be growing old together.

The sharp pain of these hard realities is only slightly softened by the heightened awareness that each day is a precious gift and that life is best lived in the moment. . . .

I don't know when. I'm not sure how I'll die. Now I wonder what will happen. What will it be like? . . . God has prepared for us a new life that is beyond our imagining. Along with St. Paul, we find comfort in the assurance that "the sufferings of this present time are not worth comparing with the glory that is to be revealed" (Romans 8).

The Bible paints various pictures of life after death. A particularly meaningful image for me these days is that of the marriage feast (Matthew 22, Luke 13). Once a week, one of my colleagues brings me Holy Communion in our home. . . . Rather than bread, we use a host, or a wafer. When the time comes to partake, he dips the wafer into the chalice. As he lifts it to my mouth, I catch a quick whiff of sacred draught, then part my lips and clench my teeth together, tearing off a tiny piece of the wine soaked wafer. While it rests on the tip of my atrophied tongue, slowly dissolving to become one with my beleaguered body, I am aware that this is the only food that I take through my mouth these days. . . . For this moment of blessed Communion, I am given a foretaste of the heavenly banquet. I am given a glimpse of what lies beyond the sufferings of this present time, a vision of myself sitting at table in the kingdom of God, my health fully restored, feasting with Christ and God's people in glory. I hope the menu includes pizza and Guinness.[13]

Shortly before his death, Chris wrote a note to someone that was included in the final issue of *For Words*, titled "Memories and Memorials," compiled by Susan. The note described a vision Chris had of Christ coming to him in the midst of utter desolation:

I had a vision last night. At the darkest, most terrifying moment of doubt I have ever known, I experienced the presence of Christ. I didn't see him in bodily form, or hear a clear human voice. But I felt a warmth, and sensed a bluish light. And the words came to me like the sound of water gently falling. I bring you healing and peace. After that, I felt such hope and love and trust, along with the assurance that everything would be all right.[14]

And then, a few days after having been put to bed for the last time, after having been surrounded by people sharing their love and good-byes, after

13. Ibid., 107–110.
14. Ibid., 121.

having been hugged and kissed by his daughter and wife, at the end of the vigil at his bedside, Chris died. Susan adds her reflections about those hours.

> On Monday June 24, I awoke with Clare beside me. I looked at Chris, in his bed perpendicular to mine, and knew he would die that day. He had entered the death coma. A blanket of peace covered our house. Our voices became quieter. Our souls became calmer. Our pace was slower. Not out of fear of Chris' dying day; rather, knowing Chris would finally be whole again.
>
> Chris died that evening after supper. I went to check on my beloved with Clare while the others lingered at the table. Clare swabbed his mouth, and I held his hand. I watched as his breathing gradually stopped. I waited. Then I said to Clare, "I think Daddy is dead now." It happened at our usual family story time.[15]

Recalling one of Chris's final entries, I mark his death here with his own words of comfort, assurance, and hope:

> One of my favourite scenes in the Bible is the book of Exodus where Moses addresses a question to God: "What is your name?" And God answers . . . "I SHALL BE THERE." Isn't that beautiful? The name of our God is "I SHALL BE THERE."
>
> From the moment of our baptism to the end of our days on earth, the name of our God is I SHALL BE THERE. When we face all the dangers and difficulties, all the hazards and hardships of life, the name of our God is I SHALL BE THERE. When we are lonely or afraid, and overwhelmed with worry and anxiety, the name of our God is I SHALL BE THERE. When we face sickness or sorrow, or heartbreak or heart ache, or even death itself—the name of our God is I SHALL BE THERE. When we face sickness or sorrow, or heartbreak or heart ache, or even death itself—the name of our God is I SHALL BE THERE. When our last breath leaves our body, and we are laid out in the grave, the name of our God is I SHALL BE THERE. And when the day of resurrection comes, with the sound of trumpets blaring, and a billion suns shimmering in a cloudless sky, the name of our God is I SHALL BE THERE.[16]

15. Ibid., 113.
16. Ibid., 110–11.

Reflecting with Chris

What can we learn about hope as surrender from Chris's story? What does it teach us? How does it relate to our definition of hope, and what does it say about care?

In hearing briefly about Chris's story in living with ALS, we can sense the extent to which any surrender he experienced was not an easy kind of giving up on life. Rather, for Chris, the movement toward surrender and acceptance was a movement that happened over and over again, and each time, it was hard fought. He describes how with each loss endured he experienced grief. He got angry, sad, overwhelmed, and sometimes depressed, and eventually he accepted it. Such acceptance not only made his life more livable but also allowed blessing to be part of his life. Sometimes his words suggest that he surrendered in spite of himself and discovered grace flowing into him in moments of miracles and wonders.[17] At other times, he was caught up in sadness and sorrow, anticipating his losses, when he would find himself met by one who unexpectedly blessed and encouraged him.[18] Through his grief and sadness, he was also given eyes to see blessings that might otherwise have been imperceptible or unrecognized. We can hear throughout *For Words* how the practice of writing and especially of serving others through his writing enabled his experiences of loss to be opened up so he could see blessing within. In some sense, his openness to face the reality of his illness, and his commitment to pursue a ministry of hope and healing through it, together reflect a pattern of the spiritual life that he lived into over and over again. In each instance, he faced head-on the trials and terrors of what his illness was doing to him: he mourned and lamented, he awaited and sought

17. On a couple of occasions Chris describes that he experienced miraculous divine encounters. One such encounter happened when he was walking to church shortly after his diagnosis. A woman who was only vaguely familiar to him approached and addressed him and began to weep and share in tongues a message given her by God. She then translated: "I am the Lord your God and you need not be afraid. I am going to reach out through you. I am going to reach out through your hands and your hands will touch many people and will bring healing to many people. And I will bring healing to you. I am the Lord your God and you need not be afraid." Ibid., 55.

18. He describes a visit to Disneyland during a time when he was still able to walk. He took a break to "people watch" and ended up watching the children and the people in wheelchairs. Caught up in sorrow at the thought of himself in a wheelchair, he abruptly discovered that he was being watched. He looked over and greeted the watcher, a little girl with long dark hair and thick glasses who was sitting in a wheelchair. Unable to speak, she responded to his greeting with joyful noises and a brilliant smile, her eyes looking deep into his. After a few moments, her mother called her to join the rest of their company, and the little girl left Chris reluctantly. "Finally," he writes, "the girl turned her chair and started to move away, but her brilliant smiling eyes stayed fixed on me until she disappeared into the crowd, leaving me sitting on the curb feeling blessed. An awareness of peace and calm inhabited my entire being." Ibid., 22.

out grace, and he shared this trust that others might be blessed through it. When this blessing happened, he was blessed again.

Not only does Chris engage some of the tough questions of suffering, prayer, healing, and the nature of God from the perspective of living deeply with these questions, he also lays open some of the tougher moments of his life for contemplation, trusting that blessing will emerge. In his writing, Chris shares his movement from struggle and fight to consent and acceptance, from anger and sadness to fullness and blessing. With each symptom, each loss of ability, each transition and change, we can sense him fully living into his grief, and through this process, an opening to blessing and grace becomes possible. As one who loved life and people fully and vigorously, Chris was not one to quietly sit back and let it all fall away. Rather, by pursuing his ministry through *For Words*, he fully committed to living to the fullest the realities of life with ALS, trusting that a larger hope and healing would emerge. Paradoxically, it was by his surrender and consent to the limits imposed by ALS that he was enabled to dive most fully into life.

In our exploration of hope as surrender through Chris's story, we can also see how hope as fight, meaning, and lament also are part of his process. He fights against an easy giving up, he fights for life in the midst of the temptations of death, he fights for faith amid temptations to fear. In his vocational embrace of *For Words*, we see how claiming meaning in the midst of adversity and making a difference in others' lives become essential aspects of his journey. Also, we sense the extent to which his process includes lament—weeping, crying, raging against the loss of so much and, through this cathartic release, being opened to blessings unforeseen. In Arthur Frank's terms, Chris's narrative would be considered a *quest narrative*, wherein "the hero" meets "suffering head on, . . . accept[s] illness and seek[s] to use it."[19] Quest narratives claim meaning over against the chaos of meaninglessness and offer transformative possibility to others through the sharing of personal stories of hope in the face of adversity. Further, in quest narratives, as in Chris's narrative, the activity of claiming one's own voice and perspective feeds a sense of agency, personhood, and purpose.

When we consider Chris's story in *For Words* as an exemplar of hope as surrender, a number of themes emerge. First, the movement to surrender or acceptance is not easy, straightforward, or a given. While we can perceive in Chris's acceptance of his illness as part of his new vocation a pattern of surrender that enables him to dig deeply into his experience of limits in order

---

19. Arthur W. Frank, *The Wounded Storyteller: Body, Illness, and Ethics* (Chicago: University of Chicago Press, 1995), 115.

to bring hope and healing to himself and others, this pattern also includes a spiritual wrestling. This wrestling is manifested in his resistance to giving up control in life, and in his struggles with darkness, fear, and anxiety that at times threaten to overwhelm him. In sharing all aspects of his journey in written form, Chris enacts his primal surrender to God through his vocation, trusting that through his honest sharing, divine energy will move, and hope, healing, and blessing will come. Indeed, at times it seems that the very act of writing brings to visibility the divine presence, which is suddenly known to have been present all along. Second, in writing about his struggles to let go control and to surrender, Chris intuitively makes a clear distinction. He does not surrender or give up control to ALS itself. Rather, he gives up control, surrenders, and entrusts himself ever more deeply to God as an act of faith. When he is able to make this shift, his eyes are opened, and he perceives the divine presence everywhere. Third, when he accepts that he cannot change particular limits that have been imposed upon him, the limits themselves often become transformed into opportunities for blessing others and himself in ways he could never have imagined. Over and over, he finds himself relocated, looking at life from a different perspective than he has known before, and his sense of gratitude and joy as well as compassion for others is opened up. Paradoxically, often when he accepts his limits, the limitlessness of grace opens up. Fourth, Chris's movement toward a spirit of surrender includes a sense of forgiveness—forgiveness of life, forgiveness of death, reconciliation with others, and gratitude for the life he has led. His movement to forgive or let go, which is part of the experience of surrender, is reflected in the lack of bitterness, resentment, anger, and hostility remaining in him. Although these states of being are part of his journey, he moves to a place of release and reconciliation with himself, with life, with God, with those whom he loves, and even with death. For Chris, as for many, a primary aspect of surrender is letting go and "forgiving" God, life, others, and ourselves for not living up to our expectations. The movement to surrender or forgiveness here means letting God, life, others, and ourselves be what and who they are, not made in our image or for our purposes. Fifth, for Chris, the movement to surrender clearly has everything to do with allowing himself to fall into the everlasting arms of God, to fall into the fullness of grace. The movement to surrender is fundamentally about faith, about Chris trusting and entrusting himself to God over and over again until at last he finds himself eternally in the everlasting arms.

We can see the extent to which Chris's story reflects our understanding of hope. While the diagnosis of ALS closes off certain horizons of meaning and participation, the journey to surrender opens up possibilities for hope that could not have been imagined ahead of time. Indeed, hope would never be known in the same way as it had been for Chris before that fateful January day. However, through his pathway to surrender, horizons of meaning and participation open up for Chris, transforming his relationships with time, with others, and with the transcendent. Multiple horizons of meaning and participation expand including his sense of vocation, his sense of connectedness with life, and his commitment to make a difference in others' lives through his own. His horizon of hope is also opened up in relation to the transcendent in his expanding need for prayer and expanding awareness of the largeness of God's mercy, love, and presence. By offering his struggles with doubt and fear at God's feet for all to see, he finds his sense of trust in God opened up, along with his expectation that God will feed hope and healing in others through him. As well, on several occasions, Chris describes growing compassion for others who struggle. He feels a deeper sense of connection with people from many walks of life.

Clearly, for Chris, care means many things. Perhaps most important for him is the community he draws together around him, both the larger community with whom he related through *For Words* and the closer community who lived with and visited him regularly. A whole group of family, friends, and caregivers walked with him, talked with him, sang with him, toileted and fed him, laughed with him, and prayed with him to the end. Central to caring for Chris was ensuring that Chris could be Chris: that his relationships would be full and robust, brimming with conversation, laughter, honesty, as they had been; that he could participate as fully as possible in life and ministry; that physical or personal aids available were accessed in order to facilitate, as much as possible, Chris's full humanity being expressed and experienced in relationship. Throughout his journey of living with ALS, Chris drew people to him and surrounded himself with people who loved him and who could challenge and be changed by him. It was with such a sense of belonging and participation together in life, worship, and friendship that Chris was cared for. While the work of caregiving could be grueling at times, the experience of caring for Chris was transformative for many who accompanied him through this time. There was a giving and receiving, a sharing, implicit in the caring relationships, and that made all the difference.

POSSIBILITIES AND LIMITS

[Hope] is entered always and only through surrender; that is, through the willingness to let go of everything we are presently clinging to. And yet

when we enter it, it enters us and fills us with its own life—a quiet strength beyond anything we have ever known.
Cynthia Bourgeault[20]

Many aspects of hope as surrender have already been covered in our discussion of Chris's story. However, we will spend some time here digging in a bit more deeply to explore the possibilities and limits of hope as surrender and to consider further the theological resonances with this narrative.

Initially, my own perception of hope as surrender was deepened through working with a Buddhist chaplain. Indeed, the Buddhist notions of non-attachment can be interpreted in terms of surrender. In opposition to *hope as fight* driven by the power of the will, so common in Western understandings, hope as surrender allows for a complete letting go and trusting what is. While the spiritual practice of surrender in both Christian and Buddhist traditions may have a similar affect, the difference between the two lies in the extent to which the act of surrender presupposes a known or knowable Divine Other. Central to both traditions is the surrendering of ego control. Many writers in the Christian traditions describe the importance of surrender in practices of contemplative prayer;[21] they consider it a letting go that is related to the relaxation of ego control and the call to rest in the relationship with God.[22] The act of surrender feeds hope to the degree that the practice engages a posture of trust and receptivity rather than defeat—often a subtle distinction. Indeed, as we saw in the discussion of Chris' story, part of his discernment was that he was not admitting defeat to ALS so much as he was trusting God in the unknown territory brought on by the limits imposed by ALS. In some of his work on hope, Donald Capps makes an interesting distinction between *trusting* and *entrusting* in the practice of hope. He agrees with most theorists on hope that trust is an essential element of hope. However, he goes on to argue that for those who believe in God or a divine presence at the center of life, deliberately

---

20. *Mystical Hope: Trusting in the Mercy of God* (Lanham, ML: Cowley, 2001), 87. Julie E. Neraas, *Apprenticed to Hope: A Sourcebook for Difficult Times* (Minneapolis: Fortress Press, 2009), 4. "Hope fills us with strength to stay present, to abide in the flow of mercy no matter what outer storms assail us. It is entered . . . through the willingness to let go of everything we are presently clinging to. And yet when we enter it, it enters us and fills us with its own life—a quiet strength beyond anything we have ever known." Roy W. Fairchild, *Finding Hope Again: A Guide to Counseling Depression* (New York: Harper and Row, 1985), 50–51.

21. Jean Stairs, *Listening for the Soul: Pastoral Care and Spiritual Direction* (Minneapolis: Fortress, 2004), 59.

22. Storm Swain, *Trauma and Transformation at Ground Zero* (Minneapolis: Fortress Press, 2011), 149.

"entrusting" ourselves and our lives to God brings an element of choice and decision that enables a more "active engagement in hoping."[23] We can see in our discussion so far how both trusting and entrusting are important aspects of hope as surrender.

Hope as surrender includes the acceptance of limits that cannot be changed. Illness and adversity impose limits on us, and central to hoping in the face of such limits is acceptance of the limits. This aspect of surrender highlights a central idea in the so-called Serenity Prayer: "God, grant me the serenity to accept the things that cannot be changed." Indeed, acceptance of limits is part of the pathway to hope in the midst of adversity, illness, and death. As acceptance of limits takes place, whole new horizons of possibility can open up, as we see in Chris's story. However, there is a caution here. In the health care context, especially in the acute-care setting, the language of surrender can be looked upon with concern and occasionally addressed by a psychiatric assessment order. No doubt shaped somewhat by the hope-as-fight assumptions so common in Western medicine, health care practitioners are concerned when a person appears too easily to accept limits that may not be limits at all. Surrender in these instances is viewed as giving up. It is not uncommon to hear exasperated practitioners anxiously exclaim, "She's giving up! She'll never get out of here!" In such cases, it appears that the relationship with life and connection to others is leaning toward despair and depression rather than hope, leaning toward death rather than life, leaning away from healing and toward greater illness. Desire for life and ongoing relatedness is not visible in these patients.

Generally speaking, in the movement toward hope as surrender, the acceptance of limits does not come easily or lightly. As life and relationships are lived and known through our bodies, the imposition of limits on our bodies cannot but challenge and cause anxiety and resistance. Part of discerning the reality and meaning of limits is to be present to the sense of crisis these limits impose. The sense of resistance that come naturally in the face of limits acts as a kind of refining fire, clarifying the character of the limits imposed and the shape that acceptance must take.

Another aspect of hope as surrender touched upon in Chris's story is the experience of forgiveness. In Chris's narrative, we focused on the movement to *forgive* God, life, others, and ourselves for not living up to expectations. This sense of forgiveness reflects a kind of letting go or surrendering of our egos—our desires, needs, and sense of self-importance—being at the center of

23. Donald Capps, "The Letting Loose of Hope: Where Psychology of Religion and Pastoral Care Converge," *Journal of Pastoral Care* 51, no. 2 (1997): 148.

the universe. Indeed, such surrender is important for the growth to maturity, whoever we are and whatever our circumstances. Adversity forces us to face this call to forgive, surrender, and let go more dramatically than a comfortable live does.

John Swinton describes at length the movement from lament to forgiveness as a movement toward surrender that hands the negating elements of life over to God.[24] Examples of what one might hand over include the disappointments in life, the judgments we carry, as well as rage and a sense of injustice carried by those who are victimized. When one who has been victimized hands over forgiveness to God, Swinton argues, the victim also moves closer to forgiveness.[25] While this is not the whole story of the possibilities of forgiveness and while it does not relate specifically to Chris's story, there is much to be said for the power of forgiveness to liberate those who have been wronged from the power of those who have wronged them. I remember the story of a woman who, as a nine-year-old child, was abducted by Pinochet's forces in Chile and tortured with cigarette burns to much of her body. When I heard her as a young adult several years later, she spoke of her journey to forgive her torturers. She described it as something she needed to do for herself, not for them. She went so far as to describe it ironically as a "selfish act." Only by forgiving her torturers was she released from her fear of them and their power over her. She was freed to live without fear and with hope. We can see here the extent to which her forgiveness involved surrendering all within her that internally bound her in a destructive relationship with her torturers. Forgiveness opens up. Revenge closes down. When we are unable to let go and surrender our rage and resentment, when we are unable to forgive, the cycle of violence is bound to be perpetuated.[26] In some sense, when we forgive, we let go and let God. We surrender our wills to love having its way with us.

Indeed, forgiveness is the crux of the whole Christian narrative and stands powerfully at the heart of the gospel. The radical forgiveness embodied and proclaimed in Jesus on the cross urges us to a place of surrender but often in life finds us in a state of resistance. How can the fullness of forgiveness be true and real? How can it really be for all? How does it relate to justice? As much as we seek to proclaim it, living it in our relationships, our families and congregations can be difficult. While vast libraries have been written on this theme, for our purposes we are just able to point to the extent to which forgiveness includes

24. John Swinton, *Raging with Compassion: Pastoral Responses to the Problem of Evil* (Grand Rapids, MI: William B. Eerdmans, 2007), 132–38.

25. Ibid., 173–74.

26. Neraas, *Apprenticed to Hope*, 123.

acts of surrender that embody and generate hope. Certainly, participating in communities of faith where forgiveness is taken seriously and is a shared journey helps enable people to trust enough to take actions toward forgiveness. In Jesus' words of forgiveness on the cross, we encounter a reordering of life and relationships that places radical and life-changing love at the center of life. These words embody a complete surrender to the power of love to reorient, liberate, and transform. When we forgive others, life, God, and our enemies, the obstacles to love fall away. Love is enabled to flow through us, energizing our identity in Christ, our communion with God and in the world, and our place as compassionate human beings in solidarity with all life around us. Hope lives here.

For Christians, another central aspect of Jesus' witness to hope as surrender is the movement of kenotic, self-emptying love present on the cross.[27] In Jesus' self-emptying surrender on the cross, we also see God's consent, acceptance, and surrender to receive and love creation as it is—broken, bruised, and incapable of faithfulness on its own accord. While it seems strange to say it, in Jesus we experience God's total surrender to love. This is not to say that God surrenders to something outside God's self, yet at some level, the Christian narrative does evoke a radical reorientation to the fullness of love and grace known distinctively in the cross of Jesus.

Finally, in Jesus' last words from the cross—"Abba, into your hands I commend my spirit"—we bear witness to the full entrusting of himself to Abba God. Not only does Jesus trust God to the end, but in these words and those spoken at the Mount of Olives, he actively entrusts and fully surrenders himself. In these words of surrender, we can hear that his cries of lament and resistance have been released and he is able to let go into the everlasting arms. All of what has been of his life, all of what is and all of what will be, is given over to Abba God. This final act of surrender is ultimately an act of hope that comes to fullness in resurrection.

CONCLUSION

In situations in which unwanted death or ending appears inevitable, what does hope-enabling care look like? As we have seen, actions of hope as surrender are hard won, purged through the encounter with mourning and lament. Care in the process of surrender often encourages forgiveness and letting go of the

---

27. See also Russell Herbert, *Living Hope: A Practical Theology of Hope for the Dying* (Werrington, UK: Epworth, 2006), 147.

residue of resentment carried within. It sometimes means supporting people to take care of unfinished business in relation to others, themselves, or God. Such unfinished business can be tended to through intentional encounters with others to right wrongs, spiritual practices, and rituals of letting go. Care in such contexts can include opportunities to stay connected and to be fully oneself with others throughout all aspects of the journey—the rough parts, the funny parts, the humiliating and scary parts. This may include the gathering of a community of people, including caregivers, brought together in the face of a death or ending to enact practical care, friendship, and a willingness to be changed by the encounter. Practices of care in this instance may include sharing in community with those saints who have gone before, who have mindfully lived their journey to the end and borne witness in song, verse, or story to the life-giving possibilities in the face of endings and death. It can include meaningful actions that bless those who come after. Such actions that project into a future, past the death or ending, embody the experience of surrender and bear witness to the larger wholeness of life within which all exists, past, present, and future. Such gestures function to open up the present moment to hope—to larger transcendent horizons of meaning and participation within which one is safe to entrust, let go, and surrender.

In exploring the contours of hope as surrender, we have raised many different ways this narrative of hope is lived and manifests our descriptive definition of hope. Through Chris's story, we have borne witness to hope as surrender and its truth in life. We have considered the importance of acceptance, trust, and actions of entrusting in the realization of hope as surrender. We have examined the temptations embedded in too easily accepting the negations and adversity in life and the importance of struggle as part of the journey to surrender. We have explored different ways surrender is related to forgiveness in terms of human expectations and the desires of the will. As well, we have considered the relationship between surrender and forgiveness in terms of the power of love to reorient and transform life, particularly as this is related to the central narrative of the Christian gospel. We have discussed the kenotic self-emptying love of God surrendered on the cross of Jesus, which calls all to give their lives that they may be reordered by love. And finally, we have held up Jesus' final words in Luke as the ultimate statement of hope as surrender in the face of death. The resurrection confirms and bears witness to hope as surrender found in the life and the cross of Jesus.

Conclusion

Hope's Hidden Presence

For in hope we were saved. Now hope that is seen is not hope. For who hopes for what is seen? But if we hope for what we do not see, we wait for it with patience.
Rom. 8:24-25

The introduction to this book identifies that the narratives of hope presented here are, in part, a response to the crisis of hope that has emerged in the Western world at the end of modernity. While some continue to warn of the loss of hope in the public sphere and to hold to a modern understanding of hope that is exclusively temporal, future focused, goal oriented, and human driven, this book has sought to bring to visibility multiple ways of recognizing hope's presence in human life. In presenting our descriptive definition and in raising up individual human narratives of hope in the face of adversity, this book seeks to inspire readers' imaginations to trust in hidden possibility when all hope seems lost. Indeed, the understanding of hope explored here functions as a hermeneutical lens whereby hope's presence may be discerned in the very midst of the trials and tribulations of life, at the very end of hope as it has been known.

Implicit in our discussion is a critique of singular, simplistic notions that narrowly prescribe hope. At the same time, in looking closely at human narratives, our discussion illustrates that hope is an embodied phenomenon, specific and particular, embedded in the very fabric of people's bodies, lives, and relationships. Hope is known and lived in multivalent interconnectivity. Sometimes recognizing its presence is difficult because hope hides behind its opposite in tears of grief or in cries of righteous anger. However, as those who follow a crucified savior, we are called to recognize hope's presence even and especially when it is most hidden.

Further, our discussion has sought to encourage those who serve as caregivers to seek out and nourish hope even and especially in moments when all hope seems lost. In each narrative, we have considered care practices that have been part of nourishing and bearing witness to hope. Care takes many forms and is unique to each relationship and community. However, in each instance, practices of care serve to open up a sense of relatedness to a larger whole, a sense of hope's presence in interconnectivity. The central practice for caregivers and those called to bear witness to hope is to discern, embody, and trust hope's possibility in any given situation. Over against isolation, disconnection, and loneliness, hope is fed when horizons are opened up, when one discovers oneself to be connected, embedded, participating in something bigger than one's own little world, so to speak. Practices of hope encourage narrative, bodily, and relational reconnectivity with oneself, others, creation, God, and time. Practices of hope require thought, dialogue, creativity, imagination, and most of all perseverance and resilient trust.

As an exercise in practical theology, this discussion has brought into dialogue the ER and the Scriptures, the deathbed and the cruciform faith, trusting that this dialogue can bear fruit for both the theology and the practice of hope. Theological renderings of hope have been challenged and deepened in conversation with the hard stuff of real life. Practices of hope have been opened up through theological reflection and reframing.

Many of the narratives of hope shared and explored in this book overlap with each other. In the narrative of hope as survival, for example, we can see the presence of hope as fight, as meaning, as lament, and so on. At the same time, each of the narratives considered in chapters 3–7 has its own nuances that open up to hope's presence and possibility in different ways. Indeed, many other narratives that may be considered can similarly manifest our definition of hope. Some areas for further exploration include hope as forgiveness, hope as belonging, and hope as gratitude, to name a few. Central to this project has been the desire to complexify and expand our imaginations when it comes to understanding and discerning hope in life. Without "prettying up" the harshness of life, these narratives invite readers to open their eyes to see hope anew—in the small steps, the daily interactions, decisions, and relationships and the ways these participate in larger interconnectivities, all of which are saturated by the mostly hidden presence of divine possibility.

While the book has focused on different manifestations of hope in individual narratives of adversity, what might our exploration of hope suggest for communities, groups, and churches that face adversity and decline, that face the end of life as it has been known? While it is not my intention to consider this topic exhaustively here, I would like to point to some possible collective manifestations and practices of hope that emerge from the definition and narratives presented thus far.

What might the contours of *hope as fight* look like in a community in decline or facing an ending? In considering this question several issues come to the fore. Most importantly, the community must seek discernment regarding what to fight against and what to fight for. Generally speaking, hope fights against temptations that lead to isolation and disconnection from larger contexts of meaning and participation. When a community faces an ending, there can be the temptation to react in ways that breed destructive tendencies within the social body; blaming, anger, helplessness, and so on can undermine relationships and blind members to the larger horizons within which they are embedded and participate. Sometimes blaming is directed outwardly at a level of governance deemed responsible for decline. In such contexts, members may feel a greater sense of connection with each other as a social body joining against a common enemy. However, this kind of dynamic ultimately undermines hope, for it is fueled by negative energy. It is fueled by the fight *against* without a clear sense of what to fight *for*. Hope must fight against temptations to blame, to close off, and to react out of fear. Rather, in a community context, hope fights for connection, relationship, and participation in larger contexts of meaning and participation: spiritual connection with God through worship and prayer; narrative connection with larger horizons of meaning shaped by Scripture, stories of the faithful, and analysis of the present; relational connection with each other that feeds a sense of belonging and integrity. Indeed, as we described in chapter 3, a central concern for the manifestation of hope as fight is discernment about what can be changed and what cannot be changed, and the wisdom to know the difference. Hope as fight means also fighting for life-giving, life-affirming ways to be in relation within community and in relation to the larger world and the currents of life.

What might the contours of *hope as meaning* look like in a community in decline or facing an ending? Central to our discussion has been a focus on raising up larger contexts of meaning and participation within which the ending is taking place. These larger contexts of meaning may be discerned in relation to God, biblical narratives, confessions of faith, and the larger social context. Further, our discussion of hope as meaning emphasizes the absolute meaningfulness of life over against the pull to meaninglessness and urges us to trust life's meaningfulness in divine providence even when we cannot discern its particular content in the moment. What are ways to honor the meaningfulness of life in a community in decline? The temptation in such situations is toward meaninglessness—a sense that nothing has mattered, a sense that because the community is coming to an end, the whole experiment has been a failure and has not made a difference. However, the call to hope in such contexts requires us to find ways to bear witness to the meaningfulness of the life of the community even and especially in the face of failure, when nothing beyond its ending is conceivable. What are practices of meaning making that bear witness to life as meaningful, practices that reverence life in all its forms, practices that point to ultimate meaning of the community and its history residing in God and in the transformative and often hidden effects in people's lives? To wrestle meaning out of situations that press toward meaninglessness in our world demands creativity and courage, faith and fortitude, and a willingness to trust and entrust ourselves to God as ultimate maker of meaning.

What might the contours of *hope as survival* look like in a community in decline or facing an ending? While this narrative does not give itself to reflection on a community facing the end of its existence, it does give itself to communities where destructive behavior on the part of leadership has undermined and violated the community's sense of integrity internally and in relation to God and the world. In situations where there has been traumatic loss in leadership, through sexual or financial indiscretion, for example, what does it mean to survive? How does hope live here? How do we point to larger horizons of meaning and participation without ignoring, denying, or silencing the pain that is part of having survived trauma? Most importantly, in the mere existence of even a remnant of the community, the possibility of new life is discerned. Where there is breath, there is the sign of life and God's possibility. Central to enacting hope as survival here may well include key practices of trauma recovery: opportunities for expressing the stories of trauma within community, enacting practices of mourning for what has been lost, reconnecting to life as a community (both internally among members and as a community with the larger world), and reorganizing communal life so as to demonstrate what has been learned through the process. Discerning the presence of hope in such situations within Christian communities must include opportunities for a deepening of theological reflection, for discerning anew the presence and possibility of God in any number of ways, and for discovering pathways to stay invested and trust again. In living out this narrative collectively, the community knows itself as having survived past that which was expected to destroy it. It begins to know itself as having been given breath and being from God each day, every day, even amid the Holy Saturday experience of having survived trauma. As the community is enabled to discover again the gift of life, the pull to death is acknowledged yet known to be held within a much larger whole of having survived. Life, rather than death, is given the last word.

What might the contours of *hope as lament* look like in a community in decline or facing an ending? Making space for lament is not easy in our world. So often, we are fearful of lament, fearful of giving in to a vast, endless pit of deep sadness and overwhelming grief, fearful that it will take over and make life unbearable. However, the Scriptures and psychology point to the healing possibility of lament. What are collective practices of hope as lament? Most importantly in this instance, it is through ritualized and structured opportunities for lament that communities may experience cathartic release and the opening to a deeper way of being in relation to each other and the larger world. In the communal cry of lament together, we bear witness to the finitude and frailty of creaturely existence and to all human-made structures of reality. In such practices, we enact a reaching out toward the divine as the true and only completion to our incompletion, the wholeness that bears our brokenness. With hope as lament, a community is called to experience itself to be reaching out beyond the immediacy of loss and knows itself to be accompanied to the depths by one who cries from the cross. In Christian terms, when we give ourselves over to lament, we participate in the groaning of the Spirit that is too deep for words, trusting that our cries are heard and that they join with all who cry out for God's reign on earth as it is in heaven.

What might the contours of *hope as surrender* look like in a community in decline or facing an ending? Central to this manifestation of hope is the act of letting go—letting go of egocentricity, letting go of the many experiences of disappointment, letting go of all that keeps us desperately seeking control. In community contexts, this includes enabling individuals or groups seeking their own end to surrender their fear and their need to steer an outcome. What are practices of communal surrender that embody and point to hope, even hidden hope? No doubt, in this case as with all the others, communal prayer, worship, study, fellowship, and rituals are central to collectively engaging people's hearts, minds, and bodies in acts of hope as surrender. Hope as surrender here means trusting God in the process and entrusting one's gifts to the process with God as helper. It means letting otherness be otherness, letting difference be what it is, and thereby manifesting trust in the One who creates in diversity and abundance. It means being receptive to God's larger story that opens up horizons of possibility and invites reconnection and reinvestment in life. Most of all, hope as surrender here means enabling a community and its members to experience itself to be held in God's everlasting arms of love and grace. It is by such postures of receptivity that hope's hiddenness may be glimpsed.

One of the gifts of participating in a Christian community is the opportunity to regularly know oneself to be connected, related, belonging to a larger whole. Further, this larger whole as the body of Christ simultaneously mirrors, represents, and embodies that which transcends and enlivens it. As members of Christian communities, we are called to discover ourselves anew, together embedded within horizons of meaning and participation beyond what the eye can see. While the experience of community can include the struggle against the temptations of tyranny, control, and fear, the opportunities for hope available in community far outweigh the pitfalls of community—and I speak of this as one who has experienced traumatically the pitfalls. It is in communities of faith that care, compassion, forgiveness, generosity, belonging, and fellowship can be enacted. It is in communities of faith that larger narratives of meaning can be shared, nourished, and lived into. It is in communities of faith that shared prayer, song, worship, and rituals can enable participation in the much larger whole of God's world and horizon of eternity. Communities of faith, in their very essence, exist to practice and feed hope. For communities struggling to hope in the face of endings, the most important practices will be discovered in communal rituals that help to embody, re-narrate, and reinterpret larger horizons of meaning, participation, and belonging; rituals that point to hidden possibility and call people to turn from fear and reactivity to a deeper trust. Besides providing words to reinterpret and re-narrate experiences of loss, communal rituals can engage other senses, moving beyond cognitive and word-structured meanings to open up the imagination through embodied actions. Claiming hope's hidden presence through communal ritual in collective worship, prayer, song, and silence affirm and participate in the mystery of God's resurrecting possibility.

The end of hope – the beginning. When everything falls apart and nothing makes sense anymore, we are invited to seek out, trust, and hold onto hope that is most often hidden behind its opposite. God's hidden hope is present today in the world, as it was at Gethsemane and Golgotha, as it was in the emptiness of Holy Saturday, and as it was in the unexpected beauty of Easter morn.

Thanks be.

Bibliography

Anderson, Megory. "Spiritual Journey with the Dying, Liminality, and the Nature of Hope." *Liturgy* 22, no. 3 (2007): 41–47.

Astrow, Alan B., Ingrid Mattson, Rabbi James Ponet, and Michelle White. "Inter-religious Perspectives on Hope and the Limits of Cancer Treatment." *Journal of Clinical Oncology* 23, no. 11 (April 10, 2005): 2569–73.

Athanasiadis, Harris. *George Grant and the Theology of the Cross.* Toronto: University of Toronto Press, 2001.

Bauckham, Richard, and Trevor Hart. *Hope against Hope: Christian Eschatology at the Turn of the Millennium.* Grand Rapids: Eerdmans, 1999.

Beck A. T., M. S. Brown, R. J. Berchick, B. L. Stewart, and R. A. Steer. "Relationship between Hopelessness and Ultimate Suicide." *Focus* 4, no. 2 (2006): 291–96, available at http://focus.psychiatryonline.org/article.aspx?articleID=50623.

Beck A. T., A. Weissman, D. Lester, and L. Trexler. "The Measurement of Pessimism: The Hopelessness Scale." *Journal of Consulting and Clinical Psychology* 42, no. 6 (1974): 861–65.

Bidwell, Duane R. "Eschatology and Childhood Hope: Reflections from Work in Progress." *Journal of Pastoral Theology* 20, no. 2 (Winter 2010): 109–127.

Bidwell, Duane R., and Donald L. Batisky. "Abundance in Finitude: An Exploratory Study of Children's Accounts of Hope in Chronic Illness." *Journal of Pastoral Theology* 19, no. 1 (Summer 2009): 38–59.

Bingaman, Kirk A. "A Pastoral Theological Approach to the New Anxiety." *Pastoral Psychology* 59 (2010): 659–70.

Bourgeault, Cynthia. *Mystical Hope: Trusting in the Mercy of God.* Lanham, MD: Cowley, 2001.

Brueggemann, Walter. *Hope within History.* Atlanta: John Knox, 1987.

———. ed. *Hope for the World: Mission in a Global Context.* Louisville: Westminster John Knox, 2001.

———. *Spirituality of the Psalms.* Minneapolis: Fortress Press, 2002.

———. *Old Testament Theology.* Nashville: Abingdon, 2008.

Burnett, Joel S. *Where Is God? Divine Absence in the Hebrew Bible.* Minneapolis: Fortress Press, 2010.

Capps, Donald. *Agents of Hope: A Pastoral Psychology*. Minneapolis: Fortress Press, 1995.

———. "The Letting Loose of Hope: Where Psychology of Religion and Pastoral Care Converge." *Journal of Pastoral Care* 51, no. 2 (Summer 1997): 139–49.

———. "An Overdue Reunion." *Pastoral Psychology* 60 (2011): 167–77.

Carrigan, Robert L. "Where Has Hope Gone? Toward an Understanding of Hope in Pastoral Care." *Pastoral Psychology* 25, no. 1 (Fall 1976): 39–53.

Carson, Verna, Karen L. Soeken, and Patricia Grimm. "Hope and Its Relationship to Spiritual Well-Being." *Journal of Psychology and Theology* 16, no. 2 (1988): 159–67.

Cayley, David. *George Grant in Conversation*. Toronto: Anansi, 1995.

Clark, Michael J. "AIDS, Death and God: Gay Liberational Theology and the Problem of Suffering." *Journal of Pastoral Counseling* 21 (Spring -Summer 1986): 40–54.

Clinebell, Howard. *Counseling for Spiritually Empowered Wholeness: A Hope-Centered Approach*. New York: Haworth, 1995.

Cohen, Richard M. *Strong in the Broken Places: Voices of Illness, a Chorus of Hope*. New York: Harper Collins, 2008.

Cooper, Terry D. *Sin, Pride and Self Acceptance: The Problem of Identity in Theology and Psychology*. Downers Grove, IL: InterVarsity, 2003.

———. *Dimensions of Evil: Contemporary Perspectives*. Minneapolis: Fortress Press, 2007.

Cooper-White, Pamela. "Suffering." *The Wiley-Blackwell Companion to Practical Theology*. Edited by Bonnie Miller-McLemore. East Susses, UK: Wiley, 2012, 23–31.

Crafton, Barbara C. *Jesus Wept: When Faith and Depression Meet*. San Francisco: Jossey-Bass, 2009.

Culp, Kristine A. *Vulnerability and Glory: A Theological Account*. Louisville: Westminster John Knox, 2010.

Delbanco, Andrew. *The Real American Dream: A Meditation on Hope*. Cambridge, MA: Harvard University Press, 1999.

Dufault, Karin, and Benita Martocchio. "Hope: Its Spheres and Dimensions." *Nursing Clinic of North America* 20 (1985): 379–91.

Ellison, Gregory C. "Late-Stylin' in an Ill-Fitting Suit: Donald Capps' Artistic Approach to the Hopeful Self and Its Implications for Unacknowledged African American Young Men." *Pastoral Psychology* 58 (2009): 477–89.

Erikson, Erik H. *Insight and Responsibility*. New York: Norton, 1964.

Fairchild, Roy W. *Finding Hope Again: A Guide for Counseling Depression.* New York: Harper and Row, 1985.

Farley, Wendy. *Tragic Vision and Divine Compassion: A Contemporary Theodicy.* Louisville: Westminster John Knox, 1990.

———. *The Wounding and Healing of Desire: Weaving Heaven and Earth.* Louisville: Westminster John Knox, 2005.

Frank, Arthur W. *The Wounded Storyteller: Body, Illness, and Ethics.* Chicago: University of Chicago Press, 1995.

———. *At the Will of the Body: Reflections on Illness.* 2nd ed. New York: Houghton Mifflin, 2002.

Frankl, Viktor E. *Man's Search for Meaning.* Rev. ed. New York: Washington Square, 1984.

Frank-Stromborg, Marilyn, and Sharon J. Olsen. *Instruments for Clinical Health-Care Research.* 3rd ed. Mississauga, ON: Jones and Bartlett, 2004.

Gadamer, Hans-Georg. *Truth and Method.* London: Sheed and Ward, 1975.

Gary, Jay. "Creating the Future of Faith: Foresighted Pastors and Organic Theologians." *Dialog* 43, no. 1 (Spring 2004): 37–41.

Gerkin, Charles V. *An Introduction to Pastoral Care.* Nashville: Abingdon, 1997.

Grant, George. *Philosophy in the Mass Age.* Toronto: University of Toronto Press, 1995, repr., 1959.

———. Technology and Empire. Toronto: Anansi, 1969.

———. *Time as History.* Toronto: University of Toronto Press, 1995.

———. Technology and Justice. Toronto: Anansi, 1986.

Grenz, Stanley J. "The Hopeful Pessimist: Christian Pastoral Theology in a Pessimistic Context." *Journal of Pastoral Care* 54 (2000): 297–322.

Griesinger, Emily, and Mark Eaton, eds. *The Gift of Story: Narrating Hope in a Postmodern World.* Waco, TX: Baylor University Press, 2006.

Groopman, Jerome. *The Anatomy of Hope: How People Prevail in the Face of Illness.* New York: Random House, 2004.

Hall, Douglas John. *God and Human Suffering.* Minneapolis: Augsburg, 1986.

———. *The Reality of the Gospel and the Unreality of the Churches.* Minneapolis: Fortress Press, 2007.

——— et al. "Hope from Old Sources for a New Century." *Hope for the World: Mission in a Global Context.* Edited by Walter Brueggemann. Louisville: Westminster John Knox, 2001, 13-26.

———. "Despair as a Pervasive Ailment." *Hope for the World: Mission in a Global Context.* Edited by Walter Brueggemann. Louisville: Westminster John Knox, 2001, 83-94.

———. *Lighten Our Darkness: Toward an Indigenous Theology of the Cross.* Revised with foreword by David J. Monge. Lima, OH: Academic Renewal, 2001.

Hall, Stephen T. "A Working Theology of Prison Ministry." *Journal of Pastoral Care and Counseling* 58, no. 3 (Fall 2004): 178-196.

Herbert, Russell. *Living Hope: A Practical Theology of Hope for the Dying.* Werrington, UK: Epworth, 2006.

Herman, Judith. *Trauma and Recovery: The Aftermath of Violence—from Domestic Abuse to Political Terror.* New York: Basic, 1997.

Herth, Kaye. "Abbreviated Instrument to Measure Hope: Development and Psychometric Evaluation." *Journal of Advanced Nursing* 17, no. 10 (1992): 1251–59.

———. "Herth Hope Index." IN-CAM Outcomes Database,1989, http://www.outcomesdatabase.org/node/612.

Holton, Jan M. "Our Hope Comes from God: Faith Narratives and Resilience in Southern Sudan." *Journal of Pastoral Theology* 20, no. 1 (Summer 2010): 67–84.

Hummel, Leonard M. *Clothed in Nothingness: Consolation for Suffering.* Minneapolis: Augsburg Fortress, 2003.

Hunsinger, Deborah van Deusen. "Bearing the Unbearable: Trauma, Gospel and Pastoral Care." *Theology Today* 68, no. 1 (2011): 8–25.

Hunter, James Davidson. *To Change the World: The Irony, Tragedy, and Possibility of Christianity in the Late Modern World.* New York: Oxford University Press, 2010.

Jacobson, Nora, and Dianne Greenley. "What Is Recovery? A Conceptual Model and Explication." *Psychiatric Services* 52, no. 4, (2001): http://ps.psychiatryonline.org/article.aspx?articleid=85752.

Jones, David Lee. "A Pastoral Model for Caring for Persons with Diminished Hope." *Pastoral Psychology* 58 (2009): 641–54.

Jones, Serene. *Trauma and Grace: Theology in a Ruptured World.* Louisville: Westminster John Knox, 2009.

Keshgegian, Flora A. *Time for Hope: Practices for Living in Today's World.* New York: Continuum International, 2006.

Kinoshita, Kanae. "For a Buddhist Chaplain in a Multi-faith Setting: Is There a Place for Hope for People Who Are Dying?" MA diss., University of Sunderland, 2007.

Kuhl, David. *What Dying People Want: Practical Wisdom for the End of Life.* New York: Public Affairs, 2002.

Kujawa-Holbrook, Sheryl A., and Karen B. Montagno, eds. *Injustice and the Care of Souls: Taking Oppression Seriously in Pastoral Care*. Minneapolis: Fortress Press, 2009.

Kwan, Simon S. M. "Interrogating 'Hope': The Pastoral Theology of Hope and Positive Psychology." *International Journal of Practical Theology* 14 (2010): 47–67.

LaMothe, Ryan. "What Hope Is There: The Enthrallment of Empire Stories." *Pastoral Psychology* 56 (2008): 481–95.

————. "Reflections on Pastoral Leadership in the Face of Cultural Communal 'Ruin.'" *Journal of Pastoral Theology* 20, no. 1 (Summer 2010): 10–21.

Lasch, Christopher. *The True and Only Heaven: Progress and Its Critics*. New York: Norton, 1991.

Lear, Jonathan. *Radical Hope: Ethics in the Face of Cultural Devastation*. Cambridge, MA: Harvard University Press, 2006.

Lee, Cameron. "Dispositional Resiliency and Adjustment in Protestant Pastors: A Pilot Study." *Pastoral Psychology* 59 (2010): 631–40.

Lester, Andrew D. *Hope in Pastoral Care and Counseling*. Louisville: Westminster John Knox, 1995.

Levy, Naomi. *Hope Will Find You*. New York: Harmony, 2010.

Lewis, Alan E. *Between Cross and Resurrection: A Theology of Holy Saturday*. Foreword by John Alsup. Grand Rapids: Eerdmans, 2001.

Lifton, Robert J. *The Future of Immortality and Other Essays for a Nuclear Age*. New York: Basic, 1987.

Louw, Daniel J. "Pastoral Care and the Therapeutic Dimension of Christian Hope." *Pastoral Sciences* 17 (1998): 81–96.

————. "Creative Hope and Imagination in a Practical Theology of Aesthetic (Artistic) Reason." *Religion and Theology* 8, nos. 3–4 (2001): 327–44.

————. "*Fides Quaerens Spem*: A Pastoral and Theological Response to Suffering and Evil." *Interpretation* 57, no. 4 (October 2003): 384–97.

————. "The HIV Pandemic from the Perspective of a *Theologia Resurrectionis*: Resurrection Hope as a Pastoral Critique on the Punishment and Stigma Paradigm." *Journal of Theology for Southern Africa* 126 (November 2006): 100–114.

Lynch, William F. *Images of Hope: Imagination as Healer of the Hopeless*. Notre Dame, IN: University of Notre Dame Press, 1974.

Malmgren, Lena. *Barbed Wire and Thorns: A Christian's Reflection on Suffering*. Peabody, MA: Hendrickson, 2007.

Manoussakis, John Panteleimon. "The Anarchic Principle of Christian Eschatology in the Eucharistic Tradition of the Eastern Church." *Harvard Theological Review* 100, no. 1 (2007): 29–46.

Marcel, Gabriel. *Homo Viator: Introduction to the Metaphysic of Hope.* Translated by Emma Crauford and Paul Seaton. South Bend, IN: St. Augustine's, 1962.

May, Gerald G. *The Dark Night of the Soul: A Psychiatrist Explores the Connection between Darkness and Spiritual Growth.* New York: Harper Collins, 2004.

Maynard, Jane F. *Transfiguring Loss: Julian of Norwich as a Guide for Survivors of Traumatic Grief.* Cleveland: Pilgrim, 2006.

McCarroll, Pam, and Thomas St. James O'Connor, and Elizabeth Meakes, "Assessing Plurality in Spirituality Definitions." *Spirituality and Health: Multidisciplinary Explorations.* Edited by Augustine Meier, Thomas St. James O'Connor, and Peter Van Latwyk. Waterloo: Wilfred Laurier University Press, 43-60.

McCarroll, Pamela R. *Waiting at the Foot of the Cross: Toward a Theology of Hope for Today.* Foreword by Douglas John Hall. Eugene, OR: Pickwick, 2014.

McGee, R. F. "Hope: A Factor Influencing Crisis Resolution." *Journal of Advanced Nursing Science* 6, no. 4 (1984): 34–44.

Menninger, Karl. "Hope." *American Journal of Psychiatry* 116 (December 1959): 481–91.

Meyer, Richard. "Integrating Cognitive Theory and Theology." *American Journal of Pastoral Counseling* 2, no. 4 (2000): 3–29.

Moltmann, Jürgen. *The Theology of Hope.* Translated by Margaret Kohl. London: SCM, 1965.

———. *In the End—the Beginning: The Life of Hope.* Translated by Margaret Kohl. Minneapolis: Fortress Press, 2004.

Neraas, Julie E. *Apprenticed to Hope: A Sourcebook for Difficult Times.* Minneapolis: Fortress Press, 2009.

Nowotny, M. L. "Assessment of Hope in Patients with Cancer: Development of an Instrument." *Oncology Nursing Forum* 16, no. 1 (1989): 57–61.

Nunn, K. P. "The Construction and Characteristics of an Instrument to Measure Personal Hopefulness." *Psychological Medicine* 26 (1996): 531–45.

O'Connor, Kathleen M. *Jeremiah: Pain and Promise.* Minneapolis: Fortress Press, 2011.

Pattison, Natalie A., and Christopher Lee. "Hope against Hope in Cancer at the End of Life." *Journal of Religion and Health* 50 (2011): 731–42.

Pembroke, Neil. "Witnessing to Hope in the Christian Community through Irony." *Pastoral Psychology* 58 (2009): 433–43.

———. *Pastoral Care in Worship: Liturgy and Psychology in Dialogue*. New York: T&T Clark, 2010.

Portier-Young, Anathea E. *Apocalypse against Empire: Theologies of Resistance in Early Judaism*. Grand Rapids: Eerdmans, 2011.

Pruyser, Paul W. "Phenomenology and the Dynamics of Hoping." *Journal for the Scientific Study of Religion* 3, no. 1 (1963): 86–96.

———. "Maintaining Hope in Adversity." *Pastoral Psychology* 35, no. 2 (Winter 1986): 120–31.

Rambo, Shelly. *Spirit and Trauma: A Theology of Remaining*. Louisville: Westminster John Knox, 2010.

Richardson, Robert L. "Where There Is Hope, There Is Life: Toward a Biology of Hope." *Journal of Pastoral Care* 54, no. 1 (Spring 2000): 75–83.

Rohr, Richard, with John Booker Feister. *Hope against Darkness: The Transforming Vision of Saint Francis in an Age of Anxiety*. Cincinnati: St. Anthony Messenger, 2001.

Root, Andrew. "A Theology of the Cross and Ministry in Our Time." *Dialog* 48, no. 2 (Summer 2009): 187–93.

———. *The Promise of Despair*. Nashville: Abingdon, 2010.

Rovers, Martin. "Development of a Holistic Model of Spirituality." *Journal of Spirituality and Mental Health* 12, no. 1 (2010): 2–24.

Snyder, C. Richard, ed. *Handbook of Hope: Theory, Measures and Applications*. Waltham, MA: Academic, 2000.

Soelle, Dorothee. *Suffering*. Minneapolis: Fortress Press, 1984.

———. *The Silent Cry: Mysticism and Resistance*. Minneapolis: Fortress Press, 2001.

———. *The Mystery of Death*. Minneapolis: Fortress Press, 2007.

Stairs, Jean. *Listening for the Soul: Pastoral Care and Spiritual Direction*. Minneapolis: Fortress Press, 2000.

Stoeber, Michael. *Reclaiming Theodicy: Reflections on Suffering, Compassion and Spiritual Transformation*. New York: Palgrave Macmillan, 2005.

Stone, Howard W. "Summoning Hope in Those Who Are Depressed." *Pastoral Psychology* 46, no. 6 (1998): 431–45.

Stone, Howard W., and Andrew Lester. "Hope and Possibility: Envisioning the Future in Pastoral Conversation." *Journal of Pastoral Care* 55, no. 3 (Fall 2001): 259–69.

Stoner, Martha H. "Measuring Hope." In Frank-Stromberg and Olsen, *Instruments for Clinical Health-Care Research*, 215–28.

Stotland, Ezra. *The Psychology of Hope*. San Francisco: Jossey-Bass, 1969.

Swinton, John. *Raging with Compassion: Pastoral Responses to the Problem of Evil.* Grand Rapids: Eerdmans, 2007.

Taylor, Charles. *A Secular Age.* Cambridge, MA: Harvard University Press, 2007.

Thornton, Sharon G. *Broken yet Beloved: A Pastoral Theology of the Cross.* St. Louis: Chalice, 2002.

Underwood, Ralph L. "Personal and Professional Integrity in Relation to Pastoral Assessment." *Pastoral Psychology* 31, no. 2 (Winter 1982): 109–117.

———. "Enlarging Hope for Wholeness: Ministry with Persons in Pain." *Journal of Pastoral Care and Counseling* 60, nos. 1–2 (2006): 3–12.

———. "Hope in the Face of Chronic Pain and Mortality." *Pastoral Psychology* 58 (2009): 655–65.

Vais, Chris. *For Words: A Journal of Hope and Healing.* Guelph, ON: Susan McLeod, 2003.

Way, Peggy. *Created by God: Pastoral Care for All God's People.* St. Louis: Chalice, 2005.

Weaver, Glenn D. "Senile Dementia and a Resurrection Theology." *Theology Today* 42 (1986): 444–56.

Weil, Simone. *Formative Writings, 1929–1941.* Edited and translated by Dorothy Tuck McFarland and Wilhelmina Van Ness. London: Routledge & Kegan Paul, 1987.

Westburg, Nancy G. "Hope in Older Women: The Importance of Past and Current Relationships." *Journal of Social and Clinical Psychology* 20, no. 3 (Fall 2001): 354–65.

Whelan, Michael. "The Human Ground of Hope: A Pastoral Reflection." *Australasian Catholic Record* 82, no. 4 (October 2005), 454–63.

Wright, N. T. *Surprised by Hope: Rethinking Heaven, the Resurrection, and the Mission of the Church.* New York: Harper Collins, 2008.

Wright, Ronald W., and Brad T. Strawn. "Grief, Hope and Prophetic Imagination: Psychoanalysis and Christian Tradition in Dialogue." *Journal of Psychology and Christianity* 29, no. 2 (Summer 2010): 148–57.

Index